We're going the wrong way again, Jim

JOYCE HODGES-HITE

To Bill & Joanne,
You were Jim's
favorite couple!
Joyce Hodges-Hite

Fulton Books, Inc.
Meadville, PA

First originally published by Fulton Books 2017

ISBN 978-1-63338-486-6 (Paperback)
ISBN 978-1-63338-487-3 (Digital)

Printed in the United States of America

I would like to acknowledge technical help from Matthew Gilpin and Art Johnson. Without them, I would not have been able to get the material to you, being the computer klutz that I am.

Also, Yolanda Wallace, a former student of mine who is now a novelist, gave me hints about what and what not to include in the body of the work. I was proud to receive their help.

1

We're going the wrong way again, Jim Hite.

It all started one day when we were headed to Atlanta on I-20, probably on the way to a week night meeting of the USATF or of the Atlanta Track Club, both of which had boards we served on. Jim was driving (as usual), and I looked up at the traffic coming east to meet us as we headed in the opposite direction. There were so many cars we couldn't count them, but traffic on our side was thin. Everybody, seemingly, was going the way we weren't, so it became a mantra thereafter: We're going the wrong way again.

Probably the traffic could be easily explained: Maybe we could go to Atlanta for an evening meeting three hours away because we were retired; maybe it was the time of day we were traveling. Whatever it was, we remarked on it on numerous trips.

With our penchant for discussing points of interest, before too long, the phrase had become a metaphor for the kind of life we lived. In many instances our style of living was diametrically opposed to what many of our friends and family thought was best for us. Jim knew my mother only a few months, but that was enough for him to have heard her repeat "There's places for people like that (us!)" and "I'm sure you can find enough places in Georgia to run without trying to go all over the world." In her mind, "the wrong way" was anywhere farther than a day's trip from home.

Then there was the running itself. Jim started running in 1978—round and round in the field behind his house. His running behavior was so unusual in Pembroke that one driver actually ran him off the road in the early morning dark and then turned around to finish the job. Jim's hiding place in the ditch was the only thing that saved him. He always said he was not competitive, but he won his first race and was bitten for good. He was justifiably proud of his accomplishments, but didn't spend time bragging about them. His running time was spent training to improve.

My own running began in 1979, but I thought I had to be competitive to justify spending all that time on the road away from home. And I bragged about what I won because I didn't want people to think I was a social misfit.

As long as we were in our forties, fifties, sixties, the running could be put down to pursuit of health or thin good looks or even medals and trophies. But once we entered our "eighth decade," there we were again—going the wrong way. Few of our friends and none of our family were still running in their seventies. The first question in our house every day was "What's your workout today?" And when we traveled, the first question asked of the innkeeper was "Where can we run?" As we aged, we slowed, but that only meant the workouts took longer.

And my mama's question: "Why can't you run closer to home?" We were seeking competition our age and titles if we could earn them. Jim took up the steeplechase on the track because fewer men his age were competing in that event (again with the wrong way). He was not content just to place because he was older; he trained hard to add to his God-given talent. I took up trail running not because I liked running through woods and over mountains with roots, ruts, and snakes but because fewer women my age were competing in that style of event. (Wrong way?)

At any rate, the favorite question asked of us by the people among whom we lived was "When are you going to quit?" When indeed!

Going hard at something most people considered a hobby also would have been deemed "the wrong way" except that was the way

Jim lived. The old saying "If it's worth doing, it's worth doing well" would have fit everything he did. And the thing is we did it together. Having been married before, both of us knew what it was like to do the "running thing" alone. Not that my first husband and his first wife didn't support our efforts, but they sent us away for the competition. And we came home and made our reports.

And to cap it off, we met literally "on the road," going in opposite directions. Running was not the only aspect of our lives which set us apart from those around us. There was, with Jim, also the glaring fact that he was a Yankee among southerners, a "damn" Yankee as he was affectionately called by the Sons of Confederate Veterans. He was a native of Toledo, Ohio, a Catholic with a very liberal point of view. He was introduced to the South when he came as chaplain to Reidsville State Prison, which, along with Lyons, Pembroke, and Claxton, certainly gave him a view of life widely divergent from his city background with its small, close-knit neighborhoods and its large Catholic high school. He loved the idea of going outside his front door and finding a coterie of backyard friends—enough to play football, baseball, or basketball without having to belong to organized leagues. However, Boy Scouts was a big deal to him—not just being a member, but becoming an Eagle Scout. If there's a plan to reach the heights, then those heights must be reached.

Jim and I were constantly comparing country life here in Georgia to his city life in Ohio. Not that I was the original type country girl myself, except when Daddy was overseas during World War II. Though I picked cotton, handed tobacco to be strung for drying, weeded gardens, and scrubbed down wooden floors, all in a home with no electricity and no indoor plumbing, I was "different" too, in a way. While everybody around me, family and friends, was in the farming business, my daddy did "public" work. I refused to accept that as a curse and rapidly assumed it meant I was superior to those around me—certainly going the wrong way here. Our only claim to social life other than family was our country church, not much better attended than some of the smaller Catholic churches in this area today. But everything was a contest—learning the most

Bible verses, picking the most cotton, making the best grades—I suppose much like climbing higher on the scale of an Eagle Scout.

Then there was our choice of career; both of us knew early what we would do. With Jim, the decision was not completely his because like Hannah in the Old Testament, Jim's mom Mildred had promised him to the Lord after she had had several miscarriages. He didn't kick against the pricks much at first. He always said he was an ideal child and only let drop a few rebellious comments. Going to seminary and then into the priesthood was her plan for him, so he did it. He apparently didn't have an easy time of it either as Latin and Hebrew were Greek to him. But he mastered the thinking process, and as it was the early '60s, that thinking led him to question some of the Church's stands on certain issues. The questioning put him at odds with the hierarchy, thus his assignment to the Catholic hinterlands of Georgia—post Vatican II.

He also mastered the counseling and teaching portion of the priesthood training, so when counseling led him to leave the priesthood and marry, it was only a matter of time and a couple more careers before he began teaching in a systematic school setting. He coached and taught everything and did it so well he was relieved of his position and took up a journalism career. But teaching called again, and he answered, retiring only because I did.

My retirement, however, came at the end of thirty years of public school. I had two first years of teaching—one right out of college and one nine years later when both my children had started school. Both years were disasters, and I was ready to throw in the towel. But with a little help from a caring principal in my third year, I finally was able to manage classes well enough to impart knowledge. Then, of course, my penchant for thinking only I was right kept me in hot water throughout my career. I'd work in one school until the principal and I locked horns, then I'd move. So of my thirty years, eight was my longest stint in any one school system. My wrong way was Jim's right way. He could get along with anybody, but I, on the other hand, forced people in authority to conform to my desires. The irony now is that many of those ideas I wanted to put into practice (and sometimes did, though without permission from on high) are being hailed as the newest and greatest since sliced bread. Of course, they were initiated by someone later and younger.

So retirement was welcome. It was the summer of the 1996 Olympics. We bought tickets to every track and field event except on the day of the marathons when we stationed ourselves on the course. Can you imagine anyone else in our little town doing that? The wrong way, Babe, was our right way.

And it still was, right up until the end of Jim's life. He loved volunteering, doing research, and working with his model train. I volunteered because he did, and both of us continued with our running and fitness regime, forever traveling for one or the other's competition.

And can you imagine the politics of a liberal Yankee priest among the conservative Tea Party types of South Georgia? When we first joined forces, I have to admit that I myself called him a "bleedin' heart" liberal because he always seemed to side with the victim or whoever was being oppressed. He did not participate in the walk in Selma, Alabama, nor the demonstrations at Fort Benning, but his heart was there. He was Democrat through and through, having worked with Jimmy Carter when he was in his journalism career and having great antipathy toward Ronald Reagan and both Bushes. How would he have felt about Mr. Trump? But it was his whole philosophy of giving, giving, giving that informed his politics. He would probably have made a great Robin Hood—taking from the rich to give to the poor.

And how does this mindset fit in with his "get along with everybody" lifestyle? It meant a lot of keeping quiet and building stress. Until me. Then he had a sounding board. We talked about politics, and we found firm enough ground to be able to converse on the subject without having to agree on everything. But, unlike our recent US Congress, we made progress. Maybe he was the one making progress, and I was the one double-stepping to come into line with his thinking. However it may be viewed, we enjoyed each other's company and were able to bring divergent thinking into a positive relationship. We complemented each other. Sometimes we likened ourselves to the ends of a rubber band. We could stretch and stretch, but our intent was always to come back together.

So in effect, being different morphed into being alike.

Politics, religion, fitness, and health careers (even personal choices) set us on the opposite side of the road, and we grew to be proud of it. Not too proud, of course, because Jim was constantly aware of what he owed for his very existence. He was proud of his accomplishments and his relationships, but he knew he didn't want to be like the Pharisee who thanked God he was not like other men. Yet he was not like other men, was he?

Jim, the newly ordained priest, with his delighted Mom

Jim's work face – while still at Statesboro High School

2

Jim Hite was a beautiful little boy, beloved as an only child usually is. He was born with club feet, which gave him a desire to do all the things it was felt he couldn't or shouldn't do. The first several years of his life after the operations on his feet, he was forced to wear heavy corrective shoes. Perhaps the removal of these shoes was the only incentive he needed to become a sportsman.

He wanted to be the best athlete, and maybe his neighborhood friends thought he was. But his high school coaches must not have concurred. All his organized sports were Catholic league sports, but he wanted to become part of varsity athletics. So he wound up in the cheerleader ranks. This led to his becoming big buddies with some great players—one of whom played college and pro basketball and was still considered one of his best friends at the time of his death.

"Ooo, Sah, Sah, Sah!
Ooo, Sah, Sah, Sah!
Hit 'em on the head with a big kielbasa!"

This still rings in my head from their chanting at the end of a memorial mass held at a Central Catholic High School reunion.

He didn't make the best grades in school, but he loved studying. When he was not outside organizing pick-up games of all kinds, he was researching numerous topics. Each of those led to a lifetime pursuit. He was obsessed with toy trains, but apparently he was also led to feel guilty about spending so much time on something that was play for play itself. He was interested in the smallest versions (the N gauge)—those which would take up less space, but which would also be the most expensive.

He was a Boy Scout, so the manual was the name of that game, building merit badge upon merit badge until he finally arrived at the top of the heap. He became an Eagle Scout, and one of his favorite memories was the hike he and his fellow Scouts took from Ft. Meigs back to their Toledo neighborhood.

They played cowboys and Indians, cops and robbers, Robin Hood, etc., through the gullies that ran between neighborhoods. He became a paragon of safety and was thus allowed to stop traffic for his classmates as they had to cross busy streets walking to and from school.

Jim Hite was an altar boy, assisting in masses before daylight several times a week, so wearing a uniform to his Catholic school was not an onerous task. In addition to his duties in the church, he also sang in the boys' choir until his voice changed. Piano lessons came easy to him until strictures about his hand and finger positions and drill exercises drove him away from it.

He had an amateur radio set and came in contact with people all over the world with his ham radio. The decoder ring he ordered from Captain Midnight was in use more than just to decipher radio messages. He and his buddies used the codes regularly in their own version of adventures. His room was a loft overlooking the back-yard of his beloved neighborhood. He never broke those ties, visiting in the homes of his old neighborhood pals on every return trip to Toledo.

Though Jim loved to study, he was not a bookworm. Physical activity always appealed to him. Therefore, he did not feel belittled by a job with the city, riding a truck and doing heavy labor eight hours per day. In his vein of honest work for an honest dollar, he didn't like the way some of the workers punched the clock and then went to breakfast in the city truck.

"I can rest in heaven," he delighted in saying.

Several jobs he held during his time at home with his parents included caddying, delivering flowers for the florist, helping customers find the perfect fit in a men's clothing and shoe store, and others. The promise made to him by his uncle that he would pay for his education beyond high school so long as Jim was earning money equal to the required amount was his incentive. One job that his mother nixed was on a Lake Erie commercial ship over one summer, and he talked often about that missed opportunity. That was probably just as well; he talked about the time he fell into the lake with a cut finger, and the pollution in the water caused the cut to become infected. And after all, it was where the Maumee River met Lake Erie that the river historically caught on fire, wasn't it?

He didn't talk much about his cheerleading for the big Catholic high school he attended, but when he did, the uptick in his voice and the sparkle in his eye spoke of his enjoyment. He was always included in the group outings of the male athletes on the teams he cheered for, and he was able to demonstrate his prowess in the sports in the CYO League.

His love-hate relationship with seminary could be seen in his diligence for order in his space and in his life. He was meticulous at cleaning after himself, ordering his day, and planning for the next. He met all his deadlines early and knew how to apportion his time so that he would have freedom when he finished. It seemed to the observer that it was not the finishing of whatever task was set for him, but the actual carrying out of the work that appealed to him. He loved the farm work and even the cooking during his novitiate in Indiana.

"Mr. Hite, can you answer this... in Latin, please, *now*!" Since his Latin was not top-notch and classes at seminary were conducted in Latin, all his study was not sufficient to make him comfortable. At least one professor took it as his personal obligation to harass Jim in class, calling on him repeatedly when he suspected Jim didn't know the answers. Classmates testified that the professor would call the roll, say good morning, and then sneer, "Mr. Hite, what are your thoughts on...," a question which had to be answered correctly and in Latin, immediately. So this limitation caused him to have to attend seminary an extra year and miss a summer of recreation baseball, a loss which he regretted the rest of his life.

After his ordination he took his family (mother and father) on a driving trip into Canada where he conducted a few masses and fulfilled his mother's wishes concerning the monastic life. She was thereafter heralded in the Catholic world since her only son had entered the priesthood. But her happiness was short-lived. Because of his liberal leanings based on all the study he had engaged in even outside of class, he became involved with a group of young people headed by a priest little older than he, who was very informal in his worship services and in his counseling sessions.

As a result, some public demonstrations followed which must have embarrassed the Catholic powers-that-be because Jim was soon sent south, not to Alabama to be involved in the freedom marches, but to the backwoods of North Carolina to work in camps which had very little contact with the outside world. He used to tell of a trip to Baltimore when the other clergy in the bus with him were openly fearful of the traffic on the major highways. But, as was Jim's wont, he loved the work, gave it all he had, and never forgot his stint there.

"Let me show you our camp in the mountains," he said one day in the 1990s when we were driving on US 64, but he couldn't. He was broken-hearted to discover the lodge had been burned mysteriously and that work dismantled.

He was not yet deemed capable of being assimilated into the Church's plan, even after the liberal changes of Vatican II (a council of all Roman Catholic bishops called by Pope John XXIII to modify application of the Church's precepts), so he was sent farther onto the mission field and far enough removed from the workings of the Church to cause no harm. The prison in Reidsville, Georgia, became his next venue. The Church had fulfilled its obligation to everyday Catholics by making a great counselor of Jim Hite. However, it had failed to teach him how not to become involved, even entangled, in the lives of those he counseled. Some of the prisoners presented themselves to him as completely converted during their stay at Reidsville, and he naturally believed them. When some were released, he worked hard to help them find jobs and people to continue to help them.

When they showed their true colors and reverted to a life of crime, he found it difficult to overcome. His emotions were run through the mill during this time of his life, but seemingly he was following the path set for him by the Church. Until...

He had also been assigned a church in the area, allowing him a whole other set of parishioners who needed his help. Working with his raw emotions, he soon became embroiled in the life of one of those he was counseling. The young woman's mother was supportive of all Jim's moves, and soon the inevitable occurred. He married the girl, and they subsequently had two wonderful daughters.

A whole lifetime of family, friends, and work he convinced himself he loved stretched ahead of him. As he usually did, he threw himself, heart and soul, into this new life—becoming the perfect husband, the perfect father, the perfect son-in-law. One job he had held as part-time earlier became full-time. He was disc jockey and radio announcer extraordinaire as his voice would tell any listener whether that person was listening to him read the Bible or the sermon in church or recitations written for public occasions.

"Daddy, let me go to work with you," his daughter Jody would say in her pre-preschool years, and he'd watch her through the glass of the studio as she slept. Then his mother-in-law employed him as a lineman for the private telephone company she owned. This job eventually required his knowledge of heavy machinery and his ability to climb poles or dig trenches along with his grandfather-in-law. It also required him to leave home, much as a doctor would, to repair home lines. He used to tell of New Year's Day football games he missed because he was under someone's house in miserable conditions, repairing wires.

I was not privy to much of his life during this time: First, I didn't know him at all until a few years before his marriage ended; and second, he spoke little of the time except how happy he was with his children, how glad he was to have his parents come south to visit, how much he respected his grandfather-in-law, and how he refused to take over his wife's family's business.

Also, the years he spent in Detroit during the upheaval in the Church and during the activism for civil rights in the South will remain an unrevealed part of his life. He told me that he had shared much information about that time with his daughter, but she, not seeing what he told her as earth-shaking, has forgotten much of it.

Suffice it to say, Jim Hite was again trying to walk to the beat of his own drum, albeit within the guidelines of a strict Catholic upbringing and of a conscience bound by feelings of guilt when he experienced any kind of happiness. "I'm a Catholic," he'd say. "I can feel guilty about anything."

The present-day end of U.S. Highway 64 in North Carolina

Jim and classmate Denny O'Shea in Baton Rouge –
Denny in basketball; Jim in track and field

3

On God
Reverend Father Jim Hite
Georgia State Prison Chaplain, Reidsville, Ga.
April 1966 newsletter

"Christianity? – Christ? – So What?"

So might be worded the 20ᵗʰ century version of the question asked by Our Lord of Peter and His other disciples. "Who do men say that I am?"

Peter answered, "You are the Messiah, the Son of God."

What do you and I answer?

God has tried to tell us about Himself since time began, as recorded in the Old Testament. And finally, as if He could hold nothing more back from us, He went "all out" – He became one of us when, as God-man, He came and lived among us, among human persons; this is the core of our Christian faith, that God has become one of us!

Maybe such a fantastic fact has lost its force in our life; but it happened – He came into our world; not a neat, perfect, ordered, clickity-click world where everything is just so, but He came into and was part of our world – noisy, searching, hurting, dirty, suffering, despairing; a world as human as life itself. He was part of it, with arms and mind and heart open to those who hurt most, especially the so-called lower end of Society. The down-and-outers were at home with Him; the social outcasts, whether tax-collectors or prostitutes, were not afraid but came to Him eagerly.

When a family lost a loved one, He did what He could. When someone faked it, put on a big show, He was devastatingly blunt. And all the time, He shouted from the housetops and mountaintops, over and over, that God is a Father, not a tyrant; that human beings, each and every one, are important and of infinite value; and that, since this is so, they must love each other, or not be His followers. And because this God-man was not like men expected or wanted, most men missed Him.

So it is now. He said He would remain – and yet, as one writer (Louis Evely) has said; "With all our might we reject this God who dares differ so outrageously from the notion we'd formed of Him."

We don't see Him, for He can say to us as He said to Philip: "It's been such a long time I've been with you – and still you don't know me." In other words: "You haven't yet understood that I'm hungry and thirsty and poor; that I was where you found nothing to honor or admire, nothing to fear of reverence; that I was precisely where you felt so sure I couldn't be."

God is still hidden, until we stop making Him in our image and stop seeking Him where we think He should be. Then, when we find Him, nothing is again the same. His message is not safe, "practical," but it must stir me up – or I'm missing the point of following Christ!

He is present, here at the Georgia State Prison. You, because this God became Man also, you are of fantastic value! You are vitally important to God! God has taken man, you and me, very seriously – I cannot begin to comprehend the depths of what this means, but it is magnificent! And He has said that we are liars when we say we care about Him and do not take those around us with the same serious-ness. By Baptism, we are called to take each other as God does; to see and discover our own self-worth and value by discovering the worth and value of the persons around us – right here at Georgia State Prison. No matter what is said or done to you, you are important, you are human, you *ARE*!! Such is the "Good News of our Salvation!"

4

My life was governed by the fact that I was not an only child, thus sharing all my childhood with three brothers and sisters and numerous cousins. The family shuttled around to follow the jobs. Daddy was a construction worker—I believed the best (like his daddy before him). He was only nineteen when he married his twenty-four-year-old wife, thus incurring the wrath of his mother toward not him, but his wife for "robbing the cradle." Early life was characterized by living away from his home town of Vidalia, Georgia, back to it, away again, back to it, *et cetera*. One running theme throughout the relationship, however, was Daddy's penchant for not coming home when he promised to, and Mama's nagging him about that. Until his daddy took us two girls to church, we'd never attended. The first boy was born when I was five. As it turns out, Daddy received his draft call before Edward was born. He evaded the Army draft by joining the Marines, a longer enlistment period. To avoid the uncomfortable situation with his mother, the family was carted off to her mother's home place in Screven County, deep in the rural South Georgia country. But this was really a boon in the long run. And it was the long run, lasting more than two years—the formative years as many refer to them. It was the middle of my first grade when Daddy left and nearly all of fourth grade when he returned. Being the country girl in a city-versus-rural first grade class led to a lasting grasp of an unconfessed class system and a spurt in the growth of an already competitive nature. I also learned that if you're the best or nearly the best at your lessons, classmates' behavior can be ignored.

Though Daddy was off at war, letters were so redacted, and Uncle Bish's radio was so temperamental; knowledge of the war was negligible. The only line that stuck was "Eat everything on your plate; children all over the world are starving." I never could figure out how my eating habits would affect those children, but...

Sure enough, when Daddy returned, moving became the norm once more, back home first. He had returned with even less of a sense of responsibility, thus embarrassing his own daddy who had given him work by having an affair during Mama's pregnancy. So Grandaddy found work for him in Savannah, a bigger, less familiar city. He also did not help him buy a car, so all travel—to work or to family amusement—had to be done by bus.

Once, when we had arrived late at night in a taxi from the bus station, my sister and I had sleepily made our way to bed while Mama put Harry, the new baby, to sleep.

"Where's Edward?" Mama screamed hysterically. But Daddy had no answer as he had left Edward asleep in the back window of the taxi. He was recovered later that night.

When that job was completed, it was time to move again, particularly since Grandaddy had died in the interim. This move was back to Mama's side of the family. You get the picture. Getting a job was easy. Keeping it and paying the rent turned out to be insurmountable because the money earned was spent on everything else but. By the time all four children were in school, Mama went to work herself to give her children some semblance of acceptable school clothes and groceries. But rent still went by the wayside. The family was actually evicted at one point.

However, it's not impossible to screen yourself from all the drinking, haranguing and doing without of teenage years when read-ing (even becoming a bookworm), excelling in school, establishing a church-going routine, and dreaming of a future which you can con-trol inform your life. Systems, schedules, letter-writing, and constant competing can be a major motivator. Being high on the social ladder was out of the question, dating was something you read about in books, and driving a car on a regular basis—all necessities for teenagers in the '50s—were denied to me. So every day was actually one more step until tomorrow.

And when tomorrow came, I was just as irresponsible as Daddy, though in different areas. The very idea of promising to have something done by a certain time and following through on that promise was alien. It would take a tome-like catalogue to list all the unfulfilled tasks. It was actually strange what I chose to honor on the list. For example, I would wait until 11:45 a.m. to jump up from the book I was reading to cook the lunch planned by Mama who was coming home to eat. The glaring disaster on this list would be the dry black-eyed peas that were put in the pot at 11:45 a.m. to be served by 12:15 p.m. Uh-oh!

But I would rise at 5:00 a.m. to translate my friends' Latin assignments for them by school time. There appeared to be no rhyme or reason for the choices of requests to be honored. It wasn't until much later during my first marriage that I seemed to grasp the concept of others depending on you for a job or a deadline.

Reading (and procrastination) may have been the culprit or, as Robert Penn Warren put it, a time thief, but the reading was what gave me opportunities to ace standardized tests of all sorts. And choice of reading material enhanced that ability as mine was mostly nineteenth century literature, which was notoriously grammatically correct.

So I was the obvious choice for proofreader for the high school and college newspapers, though I thought of myself as a budding writer—probably because of the massive crush I had on the editor.

It was only after graduation in May that I ventured to choose a college and figure out how to get in. Not enough money to cover one quarter's tuition, but good scores on entrance exams canceled each other out. And I was allowed to complete two years of study before the guillotine came down, and I was sent home to get the money to pay off my debt—or not come back. A loan from a member of my church saved me, and another move by Daddy helped. So I was able to complete the four-year degree, something I managed in three. During my last year, I met a local boy who was on disability leave from his college, and I married him before my graduation and taught a year to help him pay for his professional degree in veterinary medicine.

Being married was not an end in itself. I must become the perfect wife and mother. The characteristics of the person we've been talking about would not a perfect housewife or mother make, so the cause was lost before it was taken up.

First, being the perfect wife and mother meant adhering to the '50s view of that paragon—the "Father Knows Best" or "Donna Reed Show" mother—who dressed perfectly, served meals beautifully and on time, balanced home life with civic and social life, and reared perfect children with understanding, patience, yet strictness and encouragement while getting along with in-laws and accepting house calls with equanimity. Not recognizable as the character so far described. Really only a ticking time bomb waiting until the two boys began school, and outside work could be pursued.

Having outside work, however, demanded a rushed trip home to alleviate the guilt of not having housework or even meals done on time. More education was necessary to make the work worthwhile for our good, and we needed good as we had already had one hiccup in our relationship by becoming too close to another couple in a neighboring town also looking for more exciting behavior in their relationship.

Another early picture at my Granny's church in
the country (pic by Cousin Daisy)

5

Both first marriages could have their own volumes, but I can only guess at much of Jim Hite's married life because both members of this relationship (Jim and Joyce) realized the present was more important than the past, so they kept mum about anything that did not directly apply to the new situation.

It was obvious that both of us were very proud of our offspring— he of his two daughters, me of my two sons. We had been interested in providing a great home life. Jim spoke often (while observing the upbringing of my grandchildren) of his nightly reading aloud to his girls at their bedtime. He spoke of coaching his wife's softball team and later of his daughter's softball and basketball teams. He spoke of his own softball playing, which must have caused him great misery with his deformed feet which he never used as an excuse. One of the daughters was not high on sports but wanted to be a ballerina. He attended unnumbered dance recitals, carried her to colleges which catered to the arts, and made sure that she experienced the culture of music and the arts. He embraced all their cousins, classmates, and friends as his own, a fact which can be verified by all the contacts still kept up with his new family later on. He consciously divided his time as evenly as possible between his daughters, coaching one athletically and encouraging the other culturally.

This particular, apparently unorthodox, paternal behavior was overlooked later by therapists who encouraged his non-athletic second daughter to blame him for her eating disorder which continued on into adulthood, despite the fact that he had spent a fortune paying for her treatment.

"I was the last to know" and "Sometimes I wonder what my friends thought of me when I displayed no knowledge of the situation" were just a couple of his repeated phrases about certain behaviors he had seen in his first wife. He seldom spoke of anything other than the good times.

The quotes were wistful rather than hate-filled, however, as he sought marriage counseling help from religious and professional personnel and, in so doing, made lasting impressions on some of the therapists and puzzled others. He was, after all, the male and was supposed to be indifferent to maintaining a relationship that seemed to be treated with casual indifference by the other party. No detailed recounting of events was ever offered, merely some quotes which would have indicated to a less naïve husband little desire to alleviate tension. For example, a comment referring to the request to take the daughters to visit their grandmother in Ohio, that they "had served their time" and didn't need to go anymore. On the other hand, a reunion of his seminary classmates which she and he had attended (during the marriage counseling period) stuck in his mind as a shining example of their happiness.

When she finally checked into a facility for addiction (more to alcohol than anything else), Jim was dumfounded, but then, this is Jim we're talking about. He never believed she was an alcoholic, but she was definitely under the influence—he thought—of the superiors in the facility and of some of the other women present. At any rate, he viewed it as a slap in the face of his attempts to heal their marriage. A six-month stay stretched into a couple of years, ending with her asking him to move out so she could return to their home alone. As was his wont, he complied, leaving things he later wished he had brought with him.

Each memory for him, however, was nostalgic. Whereas she had remembered trips to Ohio as "serving time," he remembered them fondly as if they were motor vacations. They would drive overnight, and the girls felt that they'd gone to sleep at night and waked up at their grandmother's the next morning.

He spoke of trips they'd made to Florida together, camping and cycling excursions to Jekyll Island, the Gate River Run in Jacksonville, numerous visits to Cedar Point on Lake Erie, beach trips along the Florida, Georgia, South and North Carolina coasts, and too many sports events to count.

He appreciated his mother-in-law and grandfather-in-law as he had come to them with next to nothing, worked phone lines with his grandfather-in-law, and been offered head of the company by his mother-in-law. But his training had dealt with relationships with people, so he became volunteer extraordinaire and then teacher and coach, having even greater impact on his athletes and students than he appeared to have had on his wife. He looked upon his departure as a failure, though the marriage counselor had praised him highly for his arduous, though futile attempts to repair an apparently one-sided commitment. The situation affected his health adversely. His blood pressure spiked. He had loss of sleep and appetite. His only normalcy was his running, as this was also the time of the great firing of all the coaches at Bryan County High School (even though some of them had won state championships in the same year).

When he left the house in Pembroke, he also left the town and began working for the Statesboro newspaper, throwing himself "all in" to the new job. He was a columnist but also an education reporter, and before the year was out, he was named the Georgia Association of Educators statewide winner of the School Bell award for Educational Journalism for the year 1989–90.

He may have considered himself a failure, but the general opinion was that he had acquitted himself well in everything he'd attempted: his own education, his people skills, his adaptability, his fatherhood, his volunteerism, his ethics, his athleticism.

Marriage was not something planned for his life, but he had given it his best shot.

On the other hand, I had taken what could have been a crowning achievement and had punched it full of holes. My marriage was also unplanned for—at least that soon. I was still twenty and still in college, but the marriage looked as though it would flourish. (If Jim were writing this memoir, he would also have to admit to a spotty picture of a thirty-year period of time.) My new husband was also still in school to be a veterinarian, so two years were spent in a university town where I worked to pay the bills while Eddie was still studying. But though Eddie was type 1 diabetic and said he wanted no children, I, in effect, demanded pregnancy and got it, thus curtailing my working until that child and a second were both in school—at which time I began experiencing the angst of a homebound mother and wanted to go back for another degree.

"Is this all there is?" I remember questioning myself during a walk I took one day when both children were sleeping.

Though why there was unrest is not clear: I did all the things young stay-at-home moms did—volunteer at school, join civic organizations, play bridge, sew, clean house, cook, etc. Also, during this time, we bought property where we lived in an old-timey leaky drafty house, planning for a new one. We couldn't get that, however, until I went back to work, so I sucked it up (my first failed year of teaching, that is) and went back for the appropriate degree, then began a new teaching career. The first year, again, was a disaster, but Eddie said if I couldn't work, we'd just have to forget the new house. So...

During these years, we experimented with various types of fun-producing activities without going too far afield because the veterinarian, like the doctor, needed to be available much of the time. We learned square-dancing; he tried but didn't like bridge. We went to horse frolics, horse shows, demolition derbies, movies, the beach, the mountains—all these for a day or for a weekend. Our favorite times were family picnics on the pond dam on Sunday after church followed by walks through the woods.

Then the boys' activities took over our lives—mostly sports. Whatever the boys played, and whenever they played (from midget through college) must be supported both by help in planning and by presence at all games or contests. Football was the primary suspect, baseball a close second, even some basketball. An abortive attempt at track threw that sport out the window. Golf and tennis showed up periodically, but they were indicative of the whole family's searching for some sort of physical activity which could last.

My teaching interfered somewhat after the disastrous second "first year" because I was given to understand that a total immersion in the career would be the only way possible to make a success of it. Like Jim in his commitment, however, "all in" meant edging out of some family obligations and going overboard in the students' lives—not conducive to a wonderful family atmosphere and, incidentally, leading to too much of a "good" thing.

One of the extracurricular activities that required over and above time was Y Club, but it was in this endeavor that I finally happened onto a physical activity that I have never quit. One of the four state directors had the brilliant idea that the Y Clubs could be a presence in the 1980 Peachtree Road Race, so he was trying to drum up interest. Since everything in Y Club had already captured my time and interest, why should this be different? But it was just to be a pastime, not a life, so I didn't get appropriate gear (i.e., running shoes). I added miles—up to four—in a pair of Thom McAn hiking shoes and soon became a casualty. A stress fracture of the hip grounded me; I should say "bedded" me because I was to work the next seven weeks wearing a body cast and using a hospital bed in the classroom because I couldn't sit.

I read and read even more than before, saying that I should make all that reading count. So I went back to school again. By this time, both sons were in college and Eddie had had a stroke and had cut back his veterinary practice alarmingly. I also said I would make the running work count, so I read about running, bought appropriate gear, and went back out on the roads with a vengeance.

During the next eight years, Eddie was in and out of the hospital with all sorts of diabetic complications—first the strokes, then a plantar wart which began the slide toward removal of both legs, then kidney problems leading to dialysis, and finally loss of sight. As much as possible, during the early portion of those years, we traveled to football games in Tennessee and Mississippi where the boys were playing, to high school games the boys coached after their graduation, and even to races I was participating in. Eddie particularly enjoyed our trip to Maggie Valley since it had always been one of his favorite vacation spots. After our first granddaughter Dana was born, he also enjoyed the marathon outside Tallahassee where I ran my best time, winning the race.

But he was not happy. He said his life had lost all quality, though he too went "all in." He insisted on getting prosthetic legs so he wouldn't be tied to the wheelchair. While using the wheelchair, though, he had his truck rigged with a crane and he went everywhere he could. But his last problems were too much for him, both physically and psychologically.

His funeral was held in Statesboro early on Saturday morning so that the attendees could go to the Georgia Southern football game without missing any of it.

Throughout the mourning period, a catalogue of my unnecessary behaviors, fights, arguments, and just plain nitpicking comments paraded through my mind so that I too viewed my marriage as a personal failure—at least a failure at making a happy life for someone I loved. Where's the manual?

Perhaps these are the reasons the marriage Jim and I had was anything but a failure. Both of us blamed ourselves for problems in our first unions, and by remembering our errors and working at correcting them, we would not be doomed to repeat them. Go figure.

Jim with one of his beloved trains – this one at Steamtown, Pennsylvania

Jim lounging at his family's vacation spot at Devil's Lake in Michigan

Jim's family at their last vacation at Cedar Point (pic by Joyce)

Joyce's three granddaughters – Jim thanked me for
"allowing" him to be part of that family

Jim and I at Jed's in the early 90's before our marriage

6

On Morality
Jim Hite
Millen News, May 23, 2012

"Brave New World of Dishonesty"

I found an interesting commentary in a Colleges and Universities supplement to a national publication.

It seems we've come a long way from crib notes or looking over at a fellow student's paper. The author noted that it's a "brave new world of educational dishonesty out there." The statistic quoted that 75 per cent or more of high school and college students admit to cheating. But that's not the key. It's the increasing number who think there's nothing wrong with it.

The writer, Heidi Schlumpf, a communications professor at Aurora University near Chicago, notes that she must use an online plagiarism detection site before even reading any student paper. The site compares what students submit as original with more than 90,000 periodicals and books, 200 million previously submitted student papers, and 17 billion Web pages.

She notes there are websites that offer free study guides and essays as well as services to edit the work including full revision and even tailoring the paper "to meet your instructor's expectations."

There is even a high school chat room dedicated to paper sharing and selling, to which one can add that we can be sure there are more chat rooms than only this one!

The line between research and plagiarism has become less distinct. And while educators are supposed to show students how to compose their own thoughts and then search for evidence and concrete examples, it's often the other way around. Many students, and just as many in the general population, "…don't know what they think until they've Googled it!"

Online education has been a boon for those wishing to earn a degree. However, online courses can make it easy for one student to take another student's paper, change a few words, and submit it as his own. And while the vast majority of online students do the work and earn the degree with honest effort, there are diploma and degree mills that provide the Bachelor's, Master's, and Doctorate with little more than token effort.

But what about the moral dimension?

It is cheating, pure and simple. When a student passes off another's work as his own, it is wrong. Just as when spouses or friends lie, just as when politicians or corporations lie, it is wrong.

Maybe this is one of the reasons why so many are so gullible. If a lie fits in with one's needs or prejudices, it's OK. That lie is not wrong. There is no moral dimension.

We have seen during the past several decades how a lie, told often enough, can be accepted as a fact. We see it daily in the posturing of the current political campaign.

And if we are not attuned to the moral dimension of what we do, what we say, and even what we are told, then we flounder helplessly in a mishmash of truths and falsehoods.

7

"Go, Bobby!"

I was within two miles of the end of the 10K race in my hometown of about two thousand people—Millen, Georgia. I had made a
turn to the right to run an out-and-back dogleg when, meeting me,
I saw a short white-haired guy approaching, that I had seen before
at the front of races. So I yelled, "Go, Bobby!" Bobby was a short
white-haired guy who was getting a reputation in his hometown as
the runner who never stopped. He also won a lot of races and that
was significant because he was over forty years old—a *Master*, we
called that.

However, the guy I had seen on this road was *not* Bobby, who
had already passed the incoming runners because he *was* leading the
race. This man, who was running equally beautifully and was a bet-
ter-looking version of the first short white-haired guy, turned out to
be Jim. Jim came in second, but because I had misidentified him, I'd
remember the incident. The only reason he had come to our small
race in a town fifty miles from his own was his connection to the race
director Ray Miller in a course they were taking together at Georgia
Southern.

Running was just becoming popular in the early '80s, and all of
us had to keep eyes and ears open to find races in which to compete.
Word of mouth was the best communication in those days, so when

Ray mentioned the race in Jim's town of Pembroke, we made a bee-line to enter it. Just before we arrived, I realized that I had forgotten to bring any cash. As I was signing the entry form and, with trepidation, asking whether I could write a check to cover the entry fee, up walked this short white-haired guy, and with a most disarming smile, he said, "Of course, you can write a check."

Running was our only contact, but as I became as interested in winning my age group as he and our mutual friend were, we saw each other at races frequently, particularly as long as I stayed local in my races. I believe it was my second marathon when I saw him working a water stop on my second loop around Hunter Air Force Base in Savannah, though I thought I had seen him running in the race before that. And this was my *serious* race; I was trying to qualify for Boston, and I had eyes for nothing else. I did not qualify, so I was crushed. I found out much later that Jim was crushed as well, not having been able to finish.

Fast forward several years. Both of us were married, so any contact was incidental, friendly running contact. I actually met Jim's wife during those years, his athletic daughter Jody, and the high school girl Terri he and his family had taken in—in a sort of foster relationship. But we didn't look forward to contacts; they were just inevitable when we ran the same races.

During this time, my husband of thirty years Eddie died, having suffered with the complications of type 1 diabetes such as the loss of both legs, working kidneys, and good eyesight. I had no idea what was going on in Jim's life, and I had no idea that I would ever come to care more than incidentally.

Two years following my husband's death, I began worrying about my friends' tendency to try to set me up with dates. To avoid such a happenstance, I looked around for someone fit, nice-looking, and, as it happens, younger; so I could say I was "seeing someone," no matter how inconsequential. I would be provided with an automatic excuse to avoid matchmakers. However, pickings were slim; I was over fifty after all.

Then one Saturday, I went to another race—no earth-shaking event as it was the usual Saturday fare. I just happened to know the director, and I was helping him out. I took my five-year-old grand-daughter Dana with me. That was the day Jim opened up about his personal life. He began by recounting his search for me at all the hospitality suites at the GAE state convention earlier that same week. He had been presented the School Bell award at those ceremonies, and I had gone to the dais afterward to congratulate him. But afterward I wasn't anywhere to be found in the hotel; I had in fact been staying with my sister Jenny, to whose house I'd returned immediately following the program.

After the race during the awards ceremony, the two of us sandwiched between my granddaughter and a young lady from Ohio he'd just met; he told me his wife had left him after having lived in a rehab center for more than a year before that. His conversation with the other runner gave me more information about him I had not previously known—that he also was from Ohio. I logged both bits of info but let them lie. After all, in light of my earlier searches, I thought I may have found someone else to acquaint myself with.

After failed calling attempts to invite that someone to a scheduled event (that's the way I was taught it would be acceptable to ask a member of the opposite sex to accompany you), I finally gave up on that particular project.

Approximately a month after that race, at a postconcert supper in a very nice restaurant with a romantic view of the Savannah River, three other ladies (from a chorus we were singing with) were discussing a similar subject when one of them, a widow for longer than I, remarked, "My friends are all trying to set me up with Jim Hite."

Shock, shock! I didn't know that Jim was no longer teaching in Bryan County, nor did I know he was working at the local newspaper in Statesboro where our chorus was based. Also, I didn't know he was available to be "set up." My first thought was, *I hope I haven't waited too long to call him.* That was Saturday night. Monday, I found out about a Boosters Club meeting/spring banquet at my school. When the president said members could bring husbands or significant others, I jumped at the chance and asked if I could bring someone else—a someone else he knew. He agreed, and I was on my way.

After painstakingly memorizing my speech all day, after school I went to Statesboro to run before chorus practice and called from Eddie's Aunt Audrey's house. I didn't think I could bring up our conversation of a month before, so I decided on this: "Jim, I don't know what your situation is now, but the Metter Boosters Club is having its end of year supper at a local steakhouse, and since you know Ray Tootle, the president, I was wondering if you'd like to come as my guest." Apparently, I sped through it, not giving him a chance to say anything till I finished.

And even though later he gave a different version (he said he called his daughter Jody to ask what she thought and she replied, "Go for it, Dad!"), he agreed to meet me.

He would drive from Pembroke to Metter; I would drive from Millen to Metter, and we'd meet for supper and then go home our separate ways.

Happily ever after, right? Not so because the treasurer of the organization had other plans. It was one of those quasi-cafeteria style lines that we were shuttling down, and everybody was paying up front. Just as Jim and I reached the cash register, up barged the treasurer (wife of the aforementioned president) almost yelling and using her thumb as a point-maker on the actual register, she employed her gymnasium voice to tell the cashier, "We're not paying for his meal!"

Mortified is not nearly a strong enough word to describe my feelings, and I can't imagine Jim's as he was being paid a very small salary as a newspaper reporter. It was not socially acceptable for me to offer to pay (in my mama's eyes), so I could only turn red and feel the embarrassment that weighed on me like an elephant.

It was a very uncomfortable evening as every other word was "I'm sorry!" or "Don't worry about it"—first from me and then from him.

However, that fiasco led to what happened in the next few weeks and eventually to our firm and lasting relationship. The following weekend, the chorus I was singing with had a concert to raise funds to pay for an orchestra, and along with the concert was a "low-country boil." I took Jim a ticket to the newspaper office and left it with word that if he would like, he could come to the supper, stay for the concert, and perhaps we could socialize afterward. Wonder of wonders, he *did*!

Though he was grilled while there by one of his old teaching colleagues concerning the whereabouts of his wife, we did enjoy ourselves, and when the evening was over, we again went our separate ways home.

Both of these events were on Fridays, so the following week in his duties as the covering reporter for the newspaper, he had to attend a supper—Rotary or something similar. He called and said, "It's been two Fridays in a row. Want to try for another?" I went, we enjoyed ourselves, and we went our separate ways home.

The following Friday was graduation at my school, and in light of the fact that I had coached the brother of one of the graduates, I was invited to a postceremony party at their home. I called Jim. He came, we enjoyed ourselves, and then we went our separate ways home. A charming pattern.

Even so, as I had been looking only for someone to take me to a movie, and as he still lived fifty miles from me, such meeting would not be practicable, certainly not on his salary. But we still ran, so I asked him about coming to a small race over at Midville. I picked up two of my students in Metter to come to the race and then to my house to help me with some yard work. I also planned to pick up my granddaughters Dana and Kari from their other grandmother's home on my way back and bring them to my house where my son Rex would later retrieve them. That's breakfast after the race for five people besides me. Jim was planning to go on to Savannah to meet his daughter Jody at the plane, and he had a desire to shower before he went. I lived on the way, so I offered.

Now there were six for breakfast and socializing.

But I can't leave out one important event. While we were waiting for the awards to be issued after the race, we walked down to the Ogeechee River, and under the bridge, he kissed me. I say he kissed me. He aimed to kiss me, but he missed. And all I could think about was my appearance. You've heard of a "bad hair day"? Mine was so bad I had tied it into two ponytails. I didn't look good enough to be kissed. *Oops!* On both our parts.

The breakfast later at my house was bedlam as can be imagined. I was flustered, organizing a work detail, a babysitting job, and a "boyfriend" meeting with my son. I have a hard time believing we pulled it off. That was Saturday. The following evening, the first Sunday in June, when the phone rang and it was Jim, all I could say was, "I'm so glad you called." And that was the moment I acknowledged that Jim was not just a date; he was really my boyfriend, albeit a fifty-five-year-old one.

Shortly thereafter, he moved to Statesboro as he had been offered a job back in teaching. He would continue to write for the paper until the last minute, however, and that was how he came to be still working there when I went to Australia. I had met a couple from Melbourne the year before when the Masters World Games in Eugene immediately followed the Nationals in San Diego. As they discovered I had lost my first husband the year before, they offered me an adventure of a lifetime: Come to Australia, we'll find you a marathon, and we'll show you as much as we can of our country in two weeks.

They lived up to their part of the bargain, but they didn't know I'd meet, fall in love with, and not be happy apart from Jim Hite. We traveled (the three of us—Noel, Verna, and I) from Sydney to Melbourne; some on the coast (Maruyo Heads) and some inland (Canberra). Also, as it was their winter, I've never been so cold. Outdoors, indoors, running, or walking, I shivered a lot. We even went to Ballarat, which, being inland, beat them all for cold. I'm not saying I didn't have a good time. I am saying I moped (or mooned as my mama used to say) around endlessly. I don't believe that either of them was happy in my company during those moments.

However, that two weeks, or two months as Jim later referred to it, did come to an end eventually, and I returned to a Jim Hite with a diamond ring waiting for me at the gate. I had actually anticipated the proposal. I asked a girl in the Chicago airport restroom, "Do I look good enough to be proposed to?"

So we had actually begun our relationship going the "wrong way." When two people meet and fall in love, they usually go away together following such an announcement, don't they? But I went away, and Jim went to work. Also since it was before cell phones, I spent a fortune on landline international phone calls.

Now, just because I had a diamond which everybody at my church knew I was getting because the choir director had seen Jim buying it, there could be no hurry for a wedding. I don't know whether it was Jim's idea or his mother's idea, but we began a long wait for an annulment of his first marriage. Not being privy to reasons one can get an annulment in the Catholic Church with two adult children and nearly twenty-five years of marriage, I waited calmly and patiently—adverbs that don't usually apply to my actions.

But I had learned from my first marriage mistakes that questioning one particular action can blow it out of all proportion. So I continued to wait—enough so that one of my sons (Jed) asked me right out one day, "Well, are you going to marry him or what?"

My answer: "Or what, until he gives us the go-ahead."

Over a year passed before the wedding.

In keeping with our already bizarre relationship, we had the ceremony right after church at my church on the Sunday before Thanksgiving with three ministers officiating—the Catholic priest, who had finally told us to stop waiting; my aunt, who was a minister in the Christian church; and our choir director, who was an ordained Baptist minister.

And then we worked (teaching) the next two days and took off for Atlanta for our honeymoon, running the Atlanta marathon on Thanksgiving Day. I must have been excited; I won the Masters that day.

And so it went. For the next five years, we continued to teach in different schools, neither of which was Millen that first year. But after one more year, I got a local job to finish out my thirty years of teaching, so I could retire in Millen.

And though Jim had fewer years in than I did, he left the classroom the same day I did. And thus began the era of the question, "When you retire, won't you get bored?"

Our mantra, along with "We're going the wrong way again, Jim," became "Boring would be good."

For thereafter, the whole framework of our lives was the plan: "When's your workout today?" and "What's your workout today?" And every workout was the lead up to "When's your next marathon? I need to make plans—travel plans, workout plans, my race plans—around it."

Then, "Are we running anywhere this weekend? I need to know how long or short the race is to form my workout schedule based on the type and distance of it."

It was really another job, just one whose schedule we controlled rather than having somebody control it for us.

Though both of us had been running coaches, we turned to others to help us plan our own training. I asked Benji Durden, 1980 Olympic marathoner, to help me. The first thing he told me was to stop training with Jim. And Jim turned to magazines and books, notably Jack Daniels and Hal Higdon. Both of us had some success, but there was never a question of quitting, just maybe laying off for an injury.

This lifestyle continued for the whole twenty-three years we were together.

Jim's focused racing

The men at our wedding – Dr. Charles Tuggle, psychologist who tried to help with his first marriage; Ray Miller, teacher, coach, fellow runner, and best man; Jim, the groom; my two sons, Rex Hodges and Jed Hodges

On Life
Jim Hite
Statesboro Herald, July 24, 1990

"Grab Hold of Life and Take it to the Limit"

One of the more cynical clichés of a supposedly sophisticated humorist is, "Behind every silver lining there's a cloud."

I hope there are few who really believe this. However, although I have a basically optimistic nature, I also realize there are times when even those who view the world in a positive manner find the darkness, when it comes, to be just about unbearable.

None of us can escape the "downs" of life, the valleys that can at times be so deep and dark that one wonders not only if he will get through the valley to the mountaintop, but whether the darkness itself will ever end wherever he goes.

As difficult as it is, somewhere along the line we have to come to a realization that life is not all on one level but is, rather, a roller coaster of highs and lows.

If we see this, it follows that with the right attitude, the lows can make the highs even more wonderful.

If one lives without sickness, how can he enjoy health?

If one lives without trouble, how can he enjoy smooth sailing?

If one lives without feeling pain, how can he enjoy good feelings?

For if all is constantly going well, we quickly come to take it for granted.

I wonder if a number of problems that we experience rise from trying to be shielded from what hurts. Parents, by nature, try to protect their offspring. And that is natural. But when that shielding keeps them from ever growing up through the hard knocks that are part and parcel of life, it is a different story.

It is a cliché of the coaching profession that we learn very little when we win. A good coach learns from every defeat, learns what to do to avoid the same pitfall the next time.

The same goes with winning. There are some who want to make sure they win all the time, bending rules and stacking teams and picking weak opposition to come up with a good record.

But I appreciate the comment of a top-notch high school coach I worked with for many years. He enjoyed playing above his team's classification against those that were stronger. He would say of such teams, "They help us check our oil."

While it is a natural tendency to shy away from the difficult, there is no way to avoid the difficulties and tragedies that life presents. We all have to face hardships, broken relationships, hurts that seem too deep to ever heal, and the death of our loved ones.

It does no good for a person's human growth to be always shielded from the negatives. As a teacher, I have come across parents who attempt to shield their children from the difficult, who want nothing but smooth sailing for their offspring.

But that is not the way life works. It is truly a mixed bag, with ups and downs, good things and bad. But they all work for our good, if we let them.

And that may be the key – if we let them.

There are many things that happen to us that we cannot avoid or change. It is how we accept them that makes all the difference.

Each negative can be a learning experience. Each difficulty can help us mature. Running away, being shielded from the difficult, keeps a person buried in immaturity.

Life, all of it, good and bad, positive and negative, easy and difficult, winning and losing, is meant to be sought after and embraced, for as it has been written, all things work for our good.

Remembering that, a person can live his life in an attitude of hope. There is no reason to run away, to hide. He can grab hold of life as it is and with whatever it offers, and live it to the limit.

The joy of such an attitude is just about indescribable.

9

Running, marathons for me and shorter races for Jim, was the pattern of our lives. We were more committed to it than most—certainly most who were not elite. It's not that our lives had to take a back seat but that the running life was the front and the back seat. Both of us had families, both of us were Christian and had church commitments.

Both of us worked five more years teaching and coaching between marriage and retirement. Both of us felt it was necessary to join groups of like philosophies and so began the volunteer treadmill. We traveled a lot, but very little of that travel was purely for entertainment. And even if it had been planned with entertainment in mind, a race or a volunteer opportunity would become part of the trip.

In our own personal running experiences, there figured road races of all distances, track meets, trail races, and cycling events. As for me, I made it my goal to run one hundred marathons, with competitive times, continuing to qualify for Boston as the ultimate for a Masters runner. Jim was competitive in his age group on the road, and when we took on track competition, he shopped around for something he could excel at. He found the steeplechase and continued with it until he felt he was no longer a viable competitor.

Then he turned to cycling and discovered duathlon, which he dearly loved.

Therefore, each day of our lives was structured with some form of running or workout, some form of volunteer work, and some family contact. Our weeks were governed by where we would run that weekend, which church we would attend (Baptist or Catholic or both), which family events we would be part of. Our years were organized around our big competitions (particularly those to which we traveled), our music groups, and big events in our families—birthdays, programs, ball games, graduations, reunions, etc.

Throughout all this wild, madly managed chase for our best, there was one thing that was different for both of us from our previous lives. We hated being apart. We went everywhere together. When we were working, even though coaching kept us on the job till late, Jim would call when he left Statesboro for home, and I could hardly wait for him to arrive home.

Because of this insatiable desire to share everything, each of us spent time attending things that were not necessarily the other's cup of tea. I went with him to family reunions which his ex-wife always attended, making some situations more awkward than they needed to be. Jim went with me to organizations he didn't initially want to join. Also, even today I review the countless hours he waited for me at marathon finish lines and some of them in miserable conditions. When he began the duathlon, I went with him as a spectator, so I could return the favor of waiting and cheering. But his events never lasted as long as mine had.

We traveled not all over the world, but much more than either of us had ever expected to. I think twice we went on vacations which had nothing to do with races, and only one of those was just for us. One day when he was still working, he saw a travel agent sign that read, "Jamaica for $400." He stopped the truck, went inside, and purchased tickets. We enjoyed the trip over our spring holiday so much that when the first Jamaica marathon was announced to take place in Negril some years later, he immediately signed us up, though his only race would have to be the half-marathon.

Some of our favorite memories from there include the first night when we walked across the street from our hotel to a restaurant with very few customers. They took our order by asking us what we'd like rather than bringing us a menu, then serving us as if we were the owners. They apologetically brought the ticket, at which we nearly fainted. Supper was $600. Of course, we discovered the exchange rate had inflated the price, but our first reaction was to ask where the kitchen was, so we could wash dishes.

And then in the daytime, we walked everywhere we wanted to go, even the seven miles back from the topless beach at the end of the island. It took only a couple of days for the locals to realize we preferred to walk rather than to pay a taxi driver. Still it was unnerving trying to remember which side of the road we were supposed to be on. Even running there was a hairy undertaking.

Another thing we took away from that trip was our taste for jerk chicken which lasted through our coming home, and though I'm at the bottom of the list of good cooks, I keep the seasoning on my shelves.

We took trips to conferences as well over the years, but in nearly every case, we turned those into racing or running trips. The first trip was to Bermuda, where I ran the marathon and Jim the 10K. We were new to the running scene, and we were overwhelmed to be sitting at the supper table with George Sheehan, our idol since our beginning running days. Both of us had his books on our shelves, and listening to him hold forth at the table was like reading a sequel to his books. We took it personally when he became ill later and mourned his loss as if he had been family.

In the fall after Bermuda, we went to Albuquerque for a weekend. I would run the marathon and Jim would get in some sightseeing. And luckily for him, the sights were gorgeous. The balloon festival was happening that very weekend, and when he left the hotel room, his first sighting was a large number of those huge colorful balloons in that clear high-altitude sky. I didn't see them much as my eyes are usually on the road ahead, and I don't look to right or left when I'm running; I have a fear of falling.

It was a good thing the race was on Saturday. We traveled Friday, ran Saturday, and traveled home again on Sunday. Any sightseeing I was able to join in was on Saturday afternoon. It was fortunate that the weekend was arranged that way because the previous month when I had applied for time off from my job to go to the National Masters USATF Outdoor meet in Spokane, my very enlightened new principal denied my request. "They can have a track meet without you," he'd commented.

Sure they can, and I could have a life without that person. Just to give a short picture of his understanding of life and limits: When my first husband died, my one hundred acres were part of a hunting club area handled by my next-door neighbor. This principal became part of the hunting club. I didn't. One day, my son and a friend of his were hunting in my back field when Principal showed up, confronted them, and ordered them off of his hunting club property. Luckily, this incident didn't happen until I had retired, or I may not have been able to collect my retirement checks.

In the summer, Jim and I would take longer trips, the kind you can drive over several days to reach. But the longer races were mostly in the winter months because the cold is preferable for running. So in order to keep up our school attendance and responsibilities, the weekend format above was used often. We ran in D.C., Florida, Iowa, Alabama, North and South Carolina, Virginia, Tennessee, Mississippi, Missouri, Texas, Illinois, Michigan, Minnesota, New York, Massachusetts, Maine, Connecticut, Rhode Island, California, Oregon, Nevada, Utah, Pennsylvania, Indiana, Maryland, not to speak of Ohio at least once a year, and Georgia nearly every weekend. It was a little hard to fit the Boston marathon in over a weekend since it happens on Monday, but we managed that excursion several times.

Do you see a pattern here? If the race itself was the priority, then the planning was easy: Choose the race, get the plane ticket or plan the drive, call Debbie at AAA to get the room, and Bob's your uncle. If the conference was the priority, search the calendars for a race in the area, leave the room and travel arrangements to the organization, sign up for the race, and work on merging the schedule.

Two of the most significant (for us) of the latter were the Level II Coaching School in Provo, Utah, and the USATF convention in Honolulu, Hawaii. Since we were still working, Jim's school paid for his trip to Utah. I, on the other hand (and with the above principal in mind), had to pony up my part of the expenses. Before we left on that trip, I found the Deseret Marathon and 10K in Salt Lake City, but we had made no plans to rent a car. We didn't think we'd need one as a shuttle was transporting us from SLC to Brigham Young campus, and all classes were within walking distance.

Coffee wasn't, though, because of their caffeine interdiction, and both of us developed withdrawal headaches. However, during one of our social hours, we found a person whose friend was running the race in Salt Lake City sixty miles away, and that friend was willing to pick us up at 1:30 a.m. to get us to the 5:00 a.m. start. We had to walk to town in the middle of the night where we waited patiently for our ride to show up at the running store (the wrong running store). We finally walked another block to an all-night restaurant to use a phone—it was 1992 after all—and gave our Good Samaritan our location. He patiently picked us up and took us to the race. Since he was much faster than I (he finished third overall), he arranged for someone else to drive us back to Provo.

Once back, we were given a special make-up test for the one we had missed that morning. That was the only way we would get full credit for the school. Since then, Jim and I had a soft spot in our hearts for the Mormon culture.

The Honolulu trip was one we'd talk to anybody about when we returned because of the shoestring we traveled on. It was a USATF conference one week before the Honolulu Marathon. Our flights and our hotels were comped because we were on the board of the USATF Georgia, and we had to attend all the meetings of the organization— something we would have done anyway. The only thing we had to pay for was our meals and the few extra days in the hotel—oh, and the marathon entry fee. It was a trip we were envied for, and though Hawaii was not high on my visit list, the fortuitous combination of conference and race made it really worth our while.

And what did Jim get from those extra days? Two trips to Pearl Harbor! For a person who had never served and whose father had never served in World War II, it was an emotional experience for him to visit the memorial and to participate in tours and talks with survivors. That my daddy was called up late and spent his time on Guam and not at Pearl Harbor did not dim Jim's feeling of connection with the soldiers who had died there. It was educational, but with Jim it was more; it was as if he were suffering with them.

But there were many more trips planned around races. The six more years we taught after getting together, nearly everything had to be done on weekends, and most races then were held on Saturdays. One of our shortest trips, time-wise, was to Dallas, Texas, for the White Rock Marathon and the Downtown 5000. It was the dead of winter, and our hotel had a skating rink inside. Except for all the Elvises on the course, my memories of the trip are minimal, but Jim didn't want me to forget. He bought a clock and two turtlenecks with "The Rock" emblazoned on them. Those and the ubiquitous T-shirts are constant reminders of our good times there.

I don't even remember why we went to Hampton, Virginia, but I know I ran the half-marathon on Sunday afternoon. And my name was in the age group records for a while.

We also went to Houston to run. Through my aunt, who was my one-hundred-year-old grandmother's executrix, I was able to find my long-lost sister-in-law and her children.

Jim and I met them in a downtown restaurant and had old home week, dependent on my not revealing their whereabouts to my sister, who had made a disturbing scene upon the occasion of my brother's untimely motorcycle accident and death. We struck up acquaintance, and I am still in contact with them. My nephew ran Houston as his first marathon and seemed to enjoy himself nearly as much as Jim enjoyed accompanying the rest of the family around the course.

I have to admit that it was my marathon schedule that governed most of the trips—that and marathons with accompanying shorter races. Jim had determined that the Marine Corps Marathon in 1990 had taught him all he needed to know about himself.

But he was still competitive in the shorter races. His favorite distance was the 5K, and his favorite "crowing" race was Chicago when I was fourth in my age group in the marathon and he was third in the 5K.

As soon as we retired, we made a plan which would cover the whole year and were sure it would turn out to be a winner. We planned to run the Running Journal magazine Grand Prix with something like fifteen races through the year and a point system to determine the winner. I had already participated in it previously, having placed fourth once and third once. My year was to be 1997–98; as my competition didn't do marathons, I could win—no problem. But we miscalculated how many points were given for first, and I lost the series by ten points, much closer than I had come before. At the end of the year, our reward was a cup each. We were still using the cups on a regular basis in 2013, and Jim made sure we were very careful with them. Jim called them our $4,000 cups.

We had not missed any of the races on the series, and since none of them were in Georgia, it was always at least an overnight trip and sometimes longer. What did Jim get out of it? Just by tagging along and running his best in everything but the marathon, he had gotten third place—hence the cup.

But that's the year we got involved with Atlanta Track Club and its competitive teams. They allowed me to be on the team because I was competitive in my age group. And that's how we ran the Crim Festival of Races in Flint, Michigan; the Vulcan run in Birmingham, Alabama; the Chicago Marathon; the Philadelphia Half-Marathon; and several others I had heard about but never dreamed I'd be running. And Jim loved it—the hobnobbing with the faster runners, the becoming acquainted with high-ranking coaches, and the friends he made all over the world.

Later when I became involved with USATF Georgia because Jim wanted to go to a meeting, so he could learn about officiating (he had been a baseball umpire in his previous life), the ATC powers-that-be discovered Jim's organizational acumen and wanted him to lead the ATC Masters track team. So our running also became our working. Sometimes with the organizing and carrying out of plans for the two groups, we hardly had time for our own workouts. In a way, it was a business, two full-time jobs with no remuneration. But we gained valuable experience: We could then compare the way workers in each organization were rewarded. And reward was not really a good word to describe one of them.

This work also put us on the road an inordinate amount of time. We drove everywhere. Obviously, some of the road races we traveled to needed flights, and some of the national and international track meets also required flying. But if it could be done by car, that's how we traveled. Even the train would have been Jim's preferred option, but...

Keep in mind, all this volunteering "stuff" started when we retired—I at the age of fifty-nine and Jim (just because I did) at sixty-two. We knew other fifty-nine- and sixty-two-year-olds who were retired, but we didn't know many who still participated in road races, track meets, and administrative positions for those sports. And we knew even fewer who put in the miles we did for that participation. All our local age-similar friends (small-town Georgia) were okay with participation in one or the other of the above but usually on a regional basis. Most of our regional friends were somewhat younger than we and managed participation in one or two of the areas. Our friends on a wider scale—national and worldwide—were the ones who understood what we did and were definitely younger than we.

People we knew who were our age did their traveling with tour groups or church groups. But as I've pointed out earlier, if we had been part of a tour group or a church group, or even an organizational conference, a race had to be in the area or on the day to make our trip worth the effort in our eyes.

And to make a chronological list of all those would take trolling through hours of running journals which both of us kept religiously. Before me, Jim would just write "same loop" and maybe how long it took him—a bad idea since a slower run made for a depressed day. But since I kept more detailed information, it would be possible to bore the reader with a trip-by-trip account.

Rather than that approach, however, let's try some of our more memorable adventures—some memorable for Jim and some for me. And memorable doesn't always mean good.

There's my foray into ultradistances, which usually precluded Jim's even having a race. Witness the first one—a 50K called the Fat Ass 50 in North Carolina on New Year's Day. We visited Jim's daughter Jody in Raleigh for the holiday, then drove over to Salisbury for the race. It was so laid back that Jim was allowed to drive the car beside me as long as he promised to aid any other runners he encountered. There were so few in the race, however, that he had only me to worry about. At least, in those days, his tour of duty was not so long because I could run 50K then two hours faster than I run marathons today.

Another year, there was Pittsburgh right under the stadium, back and forth on a one-and-a-half mile strip. That day, he also got to catch a cheater who turned at the drink table instead of going all the way to the end as the rest of us did.

There was Long Island where we were to run eleven loops in a park, but several of us confusedly thought it was ten and were therefore disturbed at what we thought was the end.

There was also the disaster in Indiana at the Huff Trail 50K, where Jim became very ill while I was doing three ten-mile loops. It turns out he was passing a kidney stone. There was no building to go into for warmth, the bathrooms were privies, and he was in terrible pain. Not knowing what his problem actually was kept him from telling me about it until I finished.

One of his favorite trips was a 50K in France near (ten miles from) the home of one of his cousins. He was allowed to sign up as an *accompagneur* on the course with a bike. He would have enjoyed that except for the cold rain. He became so cold before I even caught up with him at 10K where he was allowed to meet me that I had to give him my gloves. I was at least warmer than he was.

Because that race was really a 100K with only a portion of us completing only the 50K, I planned to return at a later date and run the long race. But first, I thought I should run a stepping-stone distance of fifty miles. The folks at Jim's old newspaper, the Statesboro

Herald, found out about it and set about getting a story prior to the attempt—the JFK 50-miler. I warned them, but no… At any rate, Jim was looking forward to it.

We had old home week. His daughter met us in D.C. along with the cousin from France and his daughter, and I was sent off with a bang. I had chosen that particular race purposely because it had intermediate cut-off times, and I thought it would be good to have to stop without running the whole fifty if I would not be given an official time. I didn't make the first cut-off.

So now I had to look for another race, and this time, I would look more carefully at the race course itself. I had known that some of JFK was on a railroad bed and some on the Appalachian Trail, but the Appalachian Trail I had run in Georgia was much less technical. I enjoyed myself, but there was no way for me—only an occasional trail runner, to make any time. As luck would have it, I found an ad by the same fellow who had directed my first 50K—many years previous—about a fifty-miler on the paved roads just outside Winston-Salem, North Carolina. This time, it was just Jim and me—again. He knew it would be a long day, but I'm sure he didn't know about the adventure he would have after the darkness settled in.

We were going on quiet narrow roads through a thinly populated area; I was running slightly ahead of him, facing traffic and wearing my headlamp. He was driving perhaps a couple of car-lengths behind me, so I would have a wider range of light. No cars met me, but there he was. Prime fodder for the county patrols who had been called and informed that I had a stalker. Instead of stopping him, the patrol lady came up beside me from behind and asked if he was "bothering" me. I tell you on my life I could not think of the word *husband*. I just said, "He's with me," and the lady finally understood what I meant. Obviously, finishing then was the only option, and Jim breathed a sigh of relief.

And then Jim took up a new sport—duathlon. He'd discovered in his running training that after he surpassed thirty miles per week, he began to have problems (read: *pain*) in his feet. All those years of running, mostly on his arches (the definition of flat feet) had taken their toll. So to lengthen his time working out and still ease the burden of pain, he took up bike riding. He really loved Scott Tinley's columns in USA Triathlon magazine, so he had visions of becoming a triathlete. He even took a class in Savannah, offered by one of the premiere female triathletes. But he felt he'd failed the swimming portion. He said he'd discovered he was a two-sport man, not three.

As usual, he went "all in." He entered a couple of small races, but almost immediately he found himself competing in a national championship. After all, it was in Georgia. To choose entries for international competition, USA Triathlon allotted a prorated number per age group to register. Now we're on a roll. The first world championship he participated in was Switzerland. Affoltern was our destination; since it was near Zurich, we rode the train (Jim's favorite pastime) for sightseeing. The bike ride was on the road in that competition, but the run was cross-country. And on the day of Jim's race, the rain was unrelenting. He loved the fanfare, the parade, the pre- and postrace meals, the new friends he made—many from other countries as well as from the American contingent.

Now he was officially hooked. Belgium was next, then Hungary, then Concord, North Carolina, then Ottawa in Canada. He did not win these races, and the highest he placed was fourth in Canada a few weeks before his death. But he treasured every moment of the trips—the friendships, the food, the actual competition, and the fact that I was there to cheer for him. I embarrassed him sometimes, cheering for that fellow with the "cute heinie," but he was proud I was there.

About that. We had "taught" one of our local fellows to run. He was already past forty and didn't know older people could learn that sport. In our 8K cross country race the first year we had put up mile markers, and when he saw the finish line appropriately following the fourth marker, he thought he had four more to go. He thought we'd marked Ks. So he too was hooked, and he always said he didn't really get started until around eight miles. So when he signed up for a marathon and all of us and families went, it was going to be a great day.

However, his wife and children didn't even come to the race. Jim almost cried.

Running alone is one thing; racing with no cheerleader is another.

Remember that race director from Millen I mentioned? Jim would get up at 5 a.m. even after we retired to drive into town to run with Ray before he went to work.

Those were some of Jim's happiest days. He always said he could feel superior after running before anyone else was up.

A year after Jim's heart attack in 2002, and almost ten years to the day before Jim's death, Ray wrote a piece about him that Jim kept framed and displayed by his desk.

It sums up how Ray and many other of Jim's running friends esteemed him, but Ray knew him best.

Joyce and Jim with Dan O'Brien in Mumbai

Jim attacking the steeplechase in Orono at USATF Nationals

My favorite – After Jim's race he runs in with
me at Cape Cod right after 9/11

Jim and Joyce at the end of a cross country 10K at Camp LeJeune

Jim as race director for the Magnolia Springs race
(with a little help from Claudette Sasser)

The steeple without the water

Jim studying the borrowed bike he would use to
accompany me in the 50K in Belves, France

10

Written by Ray Miller and used with permission:

Let me tell you about my friend, Jim Hite. I've been thinking about writing something about Jim since his heart attack last fall. I started thinking about something that happened last spring that really gives us a valuable insight about Jim Hite.

Jim and Joyce have been coordinating the USATF Masters Track and Field Meet at Savannah State University for several years. Jim asked me to help this year. Things can get a bit hectic during these meets, especially for the race director. One of the events was an eighty-meter hurdle race for women. Since the NCAA does not have a race of this distance, the marks for the hurdles had to be measured that morning. When the event was announced, there was only one participant. As the lady approached the starting line, she asked the starter to check the distance between the hurdles. After checking, it was discovered that the hurdles were spaced incorrectly and that we needed to get them straight. It took fifteen or twenty minutes to measure, mark, and move the hurdles. When the hurdles were set, Jim announced that the race could begin. I remember thinking that with all that trouble, I hope this lady can set a world's record. But then I thought about Jim's attitude throughout this whole ordeal. He was going to give that lady her moment in the sun; the hurdles would be placed correctly so that she could race. As he was measuring, someone approached Jim and asked if the two hundred meters had already been run. Jim, while still moving the hurdles, informed the gentleman that the two-hundred-meter race would be run on time. The gentleman said thanks and went on warming up while Jim set the last flight of hurdles. Jim walked by me and said, "I think we're ready." I knew that for two people on that track, that eighty-meter hurdle race was the most important event at that moment... the lady from Atlanta and Jim Hite.

That's the way Jim approaches everything in which he is involved. That lady had trained for this event, driven from Atlanta, registered for the event, and Jim made sure that she received the same attention and consideration as anyone at the meet—even if she was the only participant in the race.

When I first met Jim, he was coaching at Bryan County High School, and I was coaching at Jenkins County High School. We both coached girls' basketball, boys' and girls' track and boys' and girls' cross-country. Track and cross-country were called minor sports in those days. We labored in relative obscurity most of the time. But our athletes sure had a good time. There were many cross-country meets where the first and second place teams were usually Bryan County and Jenkins County. We won a few, and they won a few.

It was common for Jim and me to take our runners to area weekend races. I remember taking my team to Pembroke when Jim was director of the Pembroke Lung Run. I also remember Jim and a group from Pembroke coming to Millen to compete in our Town Square Trot road race. We took our teams to the state cross-country meet together and often stayed at the same motel. I could tell that running was very important to Jim.

Is Jim competitive? You betcha! I remember one year, our teams were scheduled to compete in a cross-country meet at Georgia Southern College. There was a 5K Road Race in Statesboro that same morning. I spoke to Jim, and we both wanted to support the 5K Race. But we couldn't because of the high school cross-country meet. We decided to enter the one-mile fun run. I remember standing at the starting line—me, Jim, and about forty little kids. The starter announced that he wanted everyone to have a good time and that this was a noncompetitive event. Yeah, right. The gun sounded, and we were off. I remember Jim and me running together for five thousand two hundred and seventy-five feet. And then it happened. About two steps from the finish line, Jim's shirt somehow got tangled in my right hand. I couldn't help but step across the finish line just a second ahead of him. Of course, Jim seems to think that maybe I grabbed him. I don't recall. But that is the only time I ever finished a race ahead of Jim—until the Hoofin' for Habitat 5K at GSU last October. More on that race in a minute.

I set my 5K personal record at a race Jim was directing in Statesboro. I took the school minibus and about twelve students over to compete in the race. I had a great race and was really excited about my time. After the race, Jim came over with a really big smile. He's coming to congratulate me on my new PR, I thought. Wrong! I remember the excitement when he announced that Joyce had invited him to the Metter Athletic Banquet the following week. I found out later that Jim had to buy his own ticket. The rest is history!

There are few honors greater than to be asked to stand beside someone at their wedding; I had the privilege of standing with Jim and Joyce on their special day. I thought at the time—and I still think—that here is truly a match made in heaven. They seemed perfect for each other. I was right.

Last year I visited Jim in Augusta after his heart surgery. I didn't know what to expect. You always worry about opening the door and seeing someone lying in bed with tubes and wires running all over the place. Not Jim. When Pat and I opened the door, Jim was in the chair beside the bed. Joyce and Jody were there, along with someone from the Augusta Running Club. Jim was preparing his workout schedule for 2003. I couldn't believe it. Well… yes I could.

I talked to Joyce a couple of days later, and she said the doctor had told Jim to begin walking in a couple of days. Oh no… Joyce told the doctor to spell out exactly how many minutes he could walk each day. She wanted to make sure that Jim knew that he was limited to ten minutes on Thursday, twelve minutes on Friday, etc. About two weeks after his surgery, I met Jim at Magnolia Springs, and I walked eighteen minutes with him. His recovery was coming along right on schedule. I remember the excitement when he talked about walking a 5K in about a month.

Remember that I said I had beaten Jim to the finish line twice? The second time was on October 18, 2002, the Hoofin' for Habitat 5K. Jim had permission from his doctor to walk the 5K. I finished the race and waited around the finish line. Joyce and several other people were there. Most of them didn't know what Jim had been through. I saw Jim coming down the home stretch. I could see by his face that he was having a tough time—not a tough time finishing the race, but a tough time walking. He wanted to *run*! He crossed the finish line, and the crowd applauded. I applauded just a little louder than everyone else (everyone except his number one cheerleader Joyce). I applauded because I got to see Jim Hite finish a race. A couple of months earlier, Jim didn't know if he would ever be able to walk three miles, and now he was almost racing again. I don't usually get goose bumps, but I did that morning. Anyway, I walked over and congratulated Jim; of course, he was disappointed in his time. But I could tell that he really enjoyed that 5K. I know I did.

I could write pages on Jim's contributions to our sport. But I can sum it up best by recounting a story I told about Jim and Joyce last summer. Jim had arranged for the Georgia Games Olympic Torch Run to come through Millen for several years. At the 2002 ceremony at the Jenkins County Courthouse, Jim and Joyce received special awards for their service to the Georgia Games. I was asked to introduce Jim and Joyce and say a few words. I told a story about a preacher who would sit beside the railroad tracks in his little town and watch the trains roll by. He would do this almost every day. One day, one of his friends asked him why he liked to sit and watch the trains. The preacher replied, "I just like to see something moving through this town that I don't have to push." That's the way Jim and Joyce are to running in Georgia. Not much moves through our running community that Jim and Joyce are not pushing.

It seems that my days of beating Jim to the finish line are over. Jim is running again, not walking. His 5K time is around twenty-five minutes, and he's working to get faster.

But just so you know, Jim, one day, I'm going to be close to you near the end of a race, and if your shirt is blowing just right and my hand accidentally gets tangled and there's nothing I can do, I might just beat you one more time. But if there is one person in this whole world that I don't mind finishing behind, it's my good buddy Jim Hite.

There is one last thing about Jim that makes him really unique in our society today. In all the years I've known him, I've never—and I really mean never—heard anyone say anything bad about Jim Hite. And that's really saying something. In closing, I just want to thank Jim for all the memories, the miles, and the great times. And here's to another sixty-nine years on the roads, my friend!

Ray Miller, 9/8/03

Jim in his Official role at Georgia Games

11

There was a TV commercial in the early 2000s that showed a groom and the men of his party gathered around a television set and not paying attention to the time. The door burst open and in rushed a harried bride dressed for her wedding, nervously seeking her groom. But when she entered and all the men awaited her castigations, she saw the TV and said, "Oh, is the game on?" and sat down to watch. One of the men commented tearily, "It's so beautiful."

Jim and I were constantly experiencing that scenario, and Jim never missed the opportunity to say, "It's so beautiful." Whereas most of the couples of our acquaintance were football watchers paired with football widows, we watched, discussed, and called the games together. We often said we should get a job announcing, which Jim had had in his life before me. And it wasn't just football; we loved baseball as well. We watched high school, college, and pro games with some slight differences in preference, but we enjoyed them all—unless our team was losing.

Though running was not covered as closely on TV, we watched marathons and track meets equally.

We came to this situation by different routes. Jim came as a coach of football, basketball, softball, and track. I came as the wife of a fan who walked the sidelines, leaving me alone in the stands with other wives who wanted to discuss anything except the game. So I learned the game in self-defense. Then my two sons played all the above sports as well as golf, so I followed them as a spectator mom until I took up running. When they became coaches, I felt that I should watch them work, so I went to as many games as was feasible. Then the granddaughters took up tennis and softball, adding a whole new facet of spectatorship.

Jim even drove to North Carolina to watch his daughter play recreational softball.

He got me involved in cycling when we got together, so that we never missed a day of the Tour de France on television and then later many other cycling events. We drove to north Georgia to watch the Tour de Georgia two years—even in the rain. And then the year it came through Millen, Jim made it his business to hustle all the townspeople out onto the streets to watch the cyclists come through. He was not successful in getting the school children out, however, as the local educational powers didn't want the school schedule disturbed by international athletes riding by in seconds.

In 1996, when the Olympics came to our state, we started a year in advance preparing. We bought tickets for every day of the competition except the days of the marathons which I wanted to view from the streets of Atlanta. It was immediately following our retirement, and from that day forward, Jim thought we needed to be involved in our sport. So we studied rules and became officials for track and field and worked meets from the Junior Olympic level through Masters in all age classifications and local competition through international meets. He was especially touched by the paralympic athletes in Atlanta, speaking of them with tears in his eyes. Jim loved being able to officiate in the language of the athlete when we worked the WAVA meet in Puerto Rico. The athletes appreciated it as well.

Jim Hite was a volunteer extraordinaire, but in the twenty-two years he lived in Millen, a town of about two thousand people, he watched others in our town get volunteer awards year after year, and he was never even nominated. That is in spite of the fact that nearly every moment of every day was dedicated to some group for which he spent hours volunteering in some way or another—either on the computer or the phone at home or on the road somewhere for some group. In other words, the groups in which he volunteered most were statewide, countrywide, nationwide, or international.

His final volunteer position was president of Friends of Magnolia Springs State Park at the same time he was president of the Augusta Choral Society Council. He was immediate past area representative of the Georgia Retired Educators Association. He had been, just two years earlier, the coordinator of the Atlanta Track Club track and field team, shepherding them for eight years through many national, area, and regional meets. He had served on the USATF-Georgia executive board for several years, attending numerous national conventions and helping to make policy affecting US representation in the Olympics.

He was multi-year meet director for USATF-GA Masters annual meets, and twice meet director for the Georgia Games. He officiated innumerable track meets throughout the area—never in Millen. Hence his being overlooked for awards locally. One of his biggest disappointments was not being chosen to run the Olympic torch here in 1996.

Jim enjoying his first grandchild Patrick

Region Track meet at Southeast Bulloch is now in
honor of Jim Hite who shot the gun there

12

We weren't different from other runners from all over the country, but we were different from other runners in our area. We were older. Also, the number of runners of any age got smaller and smaller as the area you were discussing narrowed down.

But running wasn't the only route we were taking that was different or "wrong." In social and political issues, Jim was different and, many of our local contemporaries would have said, "wrong." But at least one lady who accidentally said that in front of me learned how I felt about her criticism and later apologized. That difference was the reason for his obsession for writing columns in local newspapers. It was his chance to sound off on subjects he would not have discussed openly with just anybody.

Certain subjects which resonated one way with the locals would affect him differently, and his penchant for not hurting anyone's feelings would keep him silent. Then he would write a column on the subject, venting to a certain extent, and he could then continue his daily activities without stress. Of course, my job of proofreading also included toning down his rhetoric at times.

Some of his most covered topics included obesity and other self-imposed health problems, the high-handed behavior and high pay of certain well-known and maybe not well-respected athletes, the tendency of present-day educational systems to throw out well-established methods just because they were established, and many other topics which could be considered controversial if we had lived in an area where controversy was encouraged.

On the health question he had two mantras which he practiced and urged others to as well. Eat healthy and exercise. He brought the exercise with him when he came to me. Before he even took up running as a competitive sport, he had read Ken Cooper's book on aerobic exercise, and he ran religiously, at first round and round the pasture behind his house in the dark. He described how his running shoes would rot and wear out from the top down. But as running took hold as an accepted nonfanatic activity, he ventured to the road, mostly still in the dark. He made an effort to eat right, but coaching every high school season and playing softball and umpiring in the summer made it hard for him to get past fast foods. He lucked up when he and I got together because my first husband had been a type 1 diabetic, and all the foods I knew how to cook were for that mostly sugarless and mostly fat-free diet. I didn't junk whole categories of foods, however, so after his trouble with his gall bladder and its removal, he was back to picking and choosing even from what I cooked.

So when we walked the streets (or ran them) of our little town, it hurt him to see what looked like one out of every three people overweight or hunching along as if in pain, even at a very young age. Ours was also the era of young people using and abusing crack cocaine or even just tobacco, and as we aged and remained mostly healthy, we would watch as those young people disintegrated before our eyes.

Also, as we were in the running game, both as athletes and as coaches, we sadly had to watch runners (and others who were constantly worried about weight) abuse their bodies by either depriving themselves of food altogether or binge-eating and then throwing up what they had eaten. We saw it in our athletes and our contemporaries. They would briefly excel because of their physique and then suffer for a longer period of time following their flash of success. It became a very personal thing with Jim as one of his own children was a victim of an eating disorder.

The argument for the huge paydays of many athletes—that they were in great demand among consumers—meant nothing to Jim. He was hurt when an athlete he had respected acted out in a manner undeserving of that respect. He hated the comment made by some that the athlete was not supposed to be a role model just because he was good at a certain sport. I'm sure Jim would have thought that everyone, famous or not, should think of him/herself as a role model and act accordingly. Many of the behaviors we are seeing now with harassment of women among athletes wouldn't even exist if Jim could have had his way.

As for today's educational tendencies, don't get him started. He had absolutely no patience with the attitude that the student had to have his self-esteem promoted. There is an irony involved here. Jim was the original encourager. He never judged anyone, or as some are now differentiating between judging and being judgmental, he never was the latter. However, he felt that teachers and other education personnel overdid the compliments to the detriment of the correction of false information, so a child could sail through school thinking he was smart because he had inflated grades and complimentary comments when, in fact, he had no real education.

This attitude was prevalent among parents as well so that the student had no real grounding in fact.

The curriculum was constantly being "tampered with," according to Jim. No attempt was made, he felt, to channel the child's creativity into any accepted form. This led to the student's inability to express himself in coherent form. Though grammar was not Jim's primary problem here (it was mine), he realized misuse of words and failure to think through or reread one's work led to writing or speaking which was not coherent to any reader.

And then there was the reader who couldn't understand the difference between literal and figurative statements. Jim felt that he had been taught to think in his Catholic seminary, but then he'd been told not to. Present-day education was praising the student by giving him good marks for not thinking and then expecting him to think in his life after formal schooling. He had a whole catalogue of examples: (1) the young person in the grocery store who could scan items perfectly but had no clue how to subtract if the customer wanted to remove one item from the list, (2) the lack of ability to do without a given piece of technology—a person could not be checked into a hotel room because the computer was down, (3) the young nurse's failure to differentiate between a 1 cc vial and a .1 cc vial, (4) the person in Atlanta handling tickets for the 1996 Olympics who told the caller from New Mexico to go to the international office, (5) the person who expected the computer to do all his spell checking, *ad infinitum.*

Life, to Jim, was not a literal, well laid-out plan, but a flexible process which required adaptability. We always said we literally went the wrong way on each of our trips at least once, only to have to retrace our steps or go "sightseeing" as we worked our way back to our real destination. And sometimes our detours—or mistakes—gave us adventures we could not have planned. One of our most recent was going for a run in Callaway Gardens. What started out as a four or five miler turned into an eleven-mile morning, but we met a runner and her father (he turned out to be a maintenance overseer there). And they told us of a great out-of-the-way restaurant we would never have found on our own.

In other words, Jim was both reactive and proactive. He knew each day would have its own challenges and that we had to meet them head on. We couldn't avoid them by skirting them or by giving up, but we must make a plan and tackle whatever came our way. Our first problem together was the thirteen months we waited for his first marriage to be annulled—it never was. Luckily, we were both of the same mind about that one. Being unwilling to wait was out of the question as both of us considered our marriage worth the wait, though we didn't even live in the same town until after we married. The only problem we faced included questions about our plans, but we could answer happily because of our eager anticipation.

And being married was not only happier; it was also easier. Since I had a house, Jim moved in with me immediately after we married, and our double expenses were alleviated. We were also able to travel from home together rather than meeting first. So, in this case, two wrong ways made one right way for which we were forever thankful.

Both of us teaching and coaching was not really a problem, but it did prevent our spending as much time together as we wanted to. But since that was what we "did," neither of us had a problem with the other having to shepherd students to this or that competition, and we actually had some of the same coinciding events—the state cross-country meet and the state track meet, for example. Once we even had a dual meet, Statesboro versus Metter. And to Jim's chagrin, my Metter team beat his boys who had come in feeling the competition was beneath them (It should have been Metter was A; Statesboro was AAAA). We were not just tolerant of each other's plans with teams; we supported each other and supported each other's teams. It was an adventure neither of us had ever expected to have and which neither of us had ever experienced.

As it is with anyone else who works, our travel to Saturday or Sunday competitions for ourselves during the school year had to be crammed into the weekend. We went to Albuquerque, New Mexico, for a Sunday race by leaving on Friday, coming back on Sunday postrace and being at work on Monday morning. We did have to take a day off for the Boston marathon because it's run on Monday. Dallas, Texas, was a great December trip, but it had to be done on a similar timetable. Twin Cities in Minnesota was a weekend trip. Cleveland, Ohio, though just for the weekend, included a trip to visit Jim's mother in Toledo. The Los Angeles marathon, the Chicago marathon, the Smoky Mountain marathon, and the Las Vegas marathon all had to be timed to the last second so that the weekend could accommodate them. Luckily great races were also held on long holiday weekends, for instance, Houston, Bermuda, and Helen's Hogpen Hill Climb were all on Martin Luther King weekend.

But our summers and holiday breaks gave us opportunities to participate in events Jim gloried in and never forgot. National Masters track meets were some of his favorite trips. We did, of course, miss the one in Spokane when my principal wouldn't let me off, but others we planned enough in advance to drive. Long drives too. The summer of 1995—you remember, the hot one—we drove to East Lansing, Michigan, for the national track meet and then over to Buffalo, New York, for the Worlds. Many things were memorable about that trip, but one particularly stood out in Jim's consciousness. He called it the "international incident." When the Russian lady came into the medical area where Jim was being attended following the Steeplechase and put her arm around him complimenting him on his performance that day, I calmly removed her arm and told her in as many languages as I could use, "He's mine!" But he did enjoy it. He had also enjoyed his daughter's coming to Michigan to join us for a couple of days. He enjoyed a concert on the green on July Fourth in East Lansing, and he enjoyed being named as an official at the Buffalo meet. He didn't enjoy the Chubby Checker portion of the opening ceremonies; he didn't enjoy my broken collarbone in the first race of the week, and I don't think he enjoyed competing in the Steeplechase on the last day of the meet in pouring rain. He thought the side trip to Niagara Falls was awesome, and he laughed uproariously at my fear of going straight *up* a street (a mountain, I said) to a house where his daddy had lived as a child in Butler, Pennsylvania. Even I, who have never been hot except during a race, was miserably hot in the non-air-conditioned dormitory of SUNY Buffalo, partly because of the sling I had to wear 24/7. But we worked the meet from beginning to end and stored up the memories. I see in his files that he even saved the program.

Most of our trips, however, were taken after retirement. Though some were out of the country, we tried to experience everything we could because "we'll never get the chance to do that again." Our first was the Olympics in 1996 in Atlanta almost immediately after our retirement. We signed up and bought tickets for all track events except the days of the two marathons (I wanted to be on the streets for those). We also bought a few tickets to other events family members might want to attend. We stayed at my sister's house in Lithia Springs because she, along with many unconcerned citizens, wanted to "get out of town" for the duration. That made it very simple to drive the car one exit on I-20, park it in an all-day special Olympic facility, and ride MARTA in to the Olympic venue. You understand that means we were on our way from the stadium to board MARTA the night the bomb went off in Olympic Park. As a matter of fact, the commotion ensuing had not abated by the time we went by. Jim's daughter was on her way over from Raleigh when the news came on her radio. And in the days before cell phones, we had not arrived at my sister's yet, so obviously she was a nervous wreck when she arrived. Moments, moments...

Because Jim wanted to redeem himself for his performance in that first marathon in D.C. (or so I believed), we signed up for the ten-miler in the fall of '96, and he beat me soundly, getting his revenge for the trouncing he took in 1991 when I was under four hours in the marathon, and he was over five. This time, we enjoyed ourselves the whole weekend, but did not return there again until we took my granddaughter Kari in 2006 and later her, her boyfriend (now husband), and her sister Chelsea just before President Obama's inauguration.

The year 1997 was the London trip which Jim had researched with his British friends the Checkleys and found a local 10K and a cross country race. We went because Jim had been able to get plane tickets cheaply, and the two races coincided with our timetable. The two standouts on that trip both had to do with the races. The first was getting to the start line of the 10K, which was on a local school track somewhere on the train line just outside the city. However, there were two stops with the same name—one was a town (suburb) and the other was a soccer stadium. We didn't know until we had walked several blocks to the stadium that there was sort of a recreation league game going on which had nothing to do with a foot race. So we hurried back to the train but were unable to get back to the appropriate stop. However, we found a bus, whose driver realized we would never get to the race on time (and we had not even registered yet) if we took the usual circuitous route and walked from the bus stop. So he made an unscheduled stop and told us how to go around the fence located there and cut across an open field about five hundred yards from the back of the small stadium with the track. As we ran across the field, jerking off our warm-up suits on the way, making the world's fastest pit stop, paying to enter, and pinning on our numbers, the other runners were making their way across the track as the race was to start on the backside. Then you can imagine the scene, small race though it was: Two "Yanks" running across the infield, screaming unintelligible syllables which meant "Wait! Wait!" while the race starter is holding his gun up and hollering "Set!" Awesome day! We just kept up our pace—no "set" for us—until the 10K was over, and I even won a pair of Nike sweats. And as usual, Jim made lasting friends while he and they awaited my finish.

We were to see some of those friends the next weekend at the BVAF cross country race in Newcastle at an old slag heap turned ski slope. We should not have been allowed to compete as we weren't members nor were we even British, but the athletes all acted as if they enjoyed having us there. The competition was tough, but then they were the elite British runners, weren't they? They presented us with small plaques for participating in their race, and we met more friends whom I still count among mine today.

When we went back to Tyneside for a visit to the Checkleys (some of the Brits we had met in Edmonton and recontacted before at the above XC), they made sure we saw Hadrian's Wall, for I had asked about it before; ran on the beach of the North Sea; visited all the old churches in the area; and tried all the types of bread, which Reg could cycle out to pick up every morning. Further, Carolyn challenged Jim to a beer duel, and I couldn't tell you how many pints they downed. Carolyn could drink anyone under the table and Jim couldn't hold her a light.

Then on Sunday morning, we visited (without them) their local Church of England service, and the sermon was one Jim has written about many times—folks' tendency when they travel to "take their hometown with them." Jim always believed one couldn't learn about another's culture without viewing it with unbiased eyes. He felt that many of our friends and neighbors did just what that preacher was talking about: Everywhere they went, they took their hometown with them. That lack of communication, he thought, created a post-Babel world. If we couldn't identify with other "people groups," they could never identify with us. Though Jim may have disapproved of many behaviors he viewed in other parts of the world or even in other parts of our own country, he kept an open mind enough so that he would wind up with at least one new friend no matter where we went.

He dated his ability to be great friends with a person who had a completely opposite view of life back to his time of teaching in Bryan County and a colleague named Chuck. He spoke many times of public arguments or even practical jokes they shared so that their students could remember their relationship and their ability to disagree agreeably. When we got together, it was, in a way, continuing that sort of relationship—even in his own household. I don't know whether he even really knew how much his views and his attitude about them would affect me and my views.

What really impressed me about Jim's experiences was his tenacious hanging on to every form of souvenir he could possibly find a place for. Obviously both of us were interested in printed articles and pictures of our running exploits, but Jim saved some of everything. What will happen, for example, to his piece of the Berlin Wall? What about his grandmother's naturalization papers? What about his golf shoes from Heatherdowns, where he was a caddy for elite golfers for years? He brought home leis from Hawaii; a clock from Dallas; shirts from Kamloops; stuffed animals from Cedar Point; rosaries from Highland, Michigan; cups from Marietta, Ohio; railroad lanterns from North Carolina; picture frames and belt buckles from Albuquerque; books and DVDs from Pearl Harbor; posters from Eugene, Oregon; Mardi Gras masks from New Orleans; steins from Germany and Belgium; church bulletins and programs from every church and concert we attended. And he displayed as much or more than he could find room for. Seeing all those reminders of places we had been and friends he had made there helped him fill in any blanks in his understanding of who he was and what his purpose was.

"Did you ever think growing up in that little country Georgia town that you'd meet a boy from Ohio who'd lived a city life as an only child and who would grow up to be a priest?"

Or he would say, "I'm glad we didn't meet each other sooner. We would not have ever gotten together probably because our backgrounds were so different."

And I believe he was right. Our path through life to our meeting, our unexpected opportunity to merge our lives would have been considered highly unlikely by either of us. I remember when I had first met him he was a nice man with a nice smile, and as a race director, he let me enter his race with a check (back then cash was the way to go). But my focus that day was on the woman wearing a Boston marathon T-shirt who had just signed up in my age group. And the reason I remember her so well is that the next race I encountered her, she signed up in a different (younger) age group, so we wouldn't be competing.

That lady aside, I just remember that one moment with Jim—incidental, to say the least.

I saw him at several races after that, and he was always in a hurry to get home. What kept him from being just another runner was the fact that Ray Miller, who was from my town, counted him among his best friends. And I was working with Ray when I started running, so it was inevitable I would be at races which Jim also ran. He even brought his wife to one in Savannah, and he was always bringing his sister-in-law who looked much like his wife. He also brought Terri, one of his students whom, I later learned, he and his wife had taken in because her home life was untenable. At a race in his town once, Carolyn Lota had said to me, "Joyce, this race is yours. I'm coming off an injury." But Terri beat me that day, and Jim was very proud of her.

Then one year after I began coaching cross country, I took a team to Bryan County to run in a big meet. We never stood a chance at those big meets; my team was Class A, and the competition ranged all the way to AAAA. But he was nice to us just the same.

What I'm describing here is a purely casual running acquaintance, augmented by his amiable personality and tendency to see the good in anyone. I have recently found a note he sent me in the mail after I went to my first USATF national meet in 1987 where he congratulated me on winning the ten thousand meters. I had forgotten all about it—his note, not the race. That was also my first year running the Running Journal Grand Prix, so that was another way he knew of my exploits. But all I knew of him was what I'd see at the races we both attended.

The personality that emerged was one of caring for his family and his students plus anyone else he came in contact with. He was also interested in his own performance. I remember one comment about breaking nineteen in a 5K in Savannah on Labor Day. But his own personal accomplishments were always subjugated to those of others. He didn't travel much to races, though one of his favorites in those days was the Jacksonville River Run. The year he won a ten percenter award there loomed large on his list of running feats.

I, on the other hand, was a self-centered runner. Yes, I took my students to races. But I did it, so they could see how good I was. I soon learned that was a self-defeating activity: Three times I ran races while my students slept—in the car or in the hotel—and failed to see me finish. Not like Jim, who waited without fail at every finish line I approached.

Except one! And that was the year Michelle LaFleur qualified for the Olympic Trials at the Boston marathon. I was running in that race also—not doing so well on the day. Two of my granddaughters Dana and Kari were with Jim at the finish line, but they all three got sidetracked when Michelle came in and were unable to find their spectator spots again. So I finished then the way I have to now—alone.

But, you see, Michelle was one of his projects, and he had a few. We didn't know her until 1997, and we didn't know much about her then. All we knew was that she needed a place to live while she was preparing for the Olympic Trials. So Jim said, "We have an extra room!" We didn't know then that she had been fourteen times an NCAA All-American at Cortland State in New York. We didn't know that she would later qualify for three Olympic trials, nor that she would be named to the NCAA Hall of Fame.

That wouldn't have mattered to Jim Hite. As he had already done for a high school girl in Bryan County he had found sleeping under the stadium bleachers and another whose parents' behavior was less than desirable, he was willing to help provide shelter, even in his own home.

This was just one of the many facets of the life of Jim Hite, teacher and coach.

13

On Sport/Religion
Jim Hite
Millen News June 18, 2008

"Are Sport and Religion the Same?"

Some years ago, I discovered that one of the world's best triathletes and I share several things. No, it wasn't just that we both run
and ride a bike, albeit in far different fashion and speed. It was also
that we share a teaching career and we both write a column on a
somewhat regular basis expressing whatever insights or ideas we feel
are worth the paper, ink, and, hopefully, the time of the reader.

This triathlete/writer/teacher I've mentioned before, multiple
Ironman winner Scott Tinley. Joyce and I have owned his brand of
warm ups since we married.

Recently, Tinley wrote of a question he asked his students: Is
sport a religion? If so, why? While there is no wrong answer to this
question, he was more interested in their comments on the second
question.

Some students noticed the obvious: Sport and religion are places
of communal gathering and flow from the desire to be perfect; they
have iconic or heroic figures, detailed history, rules that inform how

followers are to act, rituals and ceremonies, and a path to personal meaning.

Others opined that sport is like a religion because the body can be used to gain some control over our surroundings, as well as distract us from more important issues.

Tinley was reading their answers when he received word of the death of a close and long-time friend. This friend was a fellow triathlete who had beaten the cancer beast into remission for years; yet it had finally returned with a vengeance.

The battle was waged once again within his friend's body with multiple bone-marrow transplants, chemotherapy, drugs. His friend fought like an endurance athlete, willing his body to work pumping the wheels of a stationary bike as he faced a poster of Lance Armstrong, until the fight was taken to a ventilator, yet continuing to struggle as an athlete struggles, enduring the pain of that struggle until he could go no further, finally in faith or something beyond naming, letting go.

Being an athlete for a very long time allows one to see other athletes come and go, their skills wax and wane and wax again, just as one's own skills do the same. But while it is inevitable that physical skills, whether speed, timing, eye-hand coordination, strength, whatever, weaken, the athlete surrenders not! The real athlete is an athlete until that final breath.

Tinley adds that sport is like a religion because it can't be anything else! With semi-faith and semi-beliefs, one will be semi-tough!

But to me, sport and religion have nothing "semi" about them.

Sport does not and will not make one religious. But sport can build the spirit that is already there, waiting and willing. Sport and religion are the same, but different.

Both give us a will to win, a will to struggle mightily to the very last breath, a will, as Paul wrote, "…to bring my body into submission, not for a crown that fades, but for one that lasts forever." Both give us a will to believe in something greater than ourselves and a will to gain power over things the spirit may always and already control.

It's something I come back to over and over. There is a mighty difference in existing and living. We're not here to take up space but to make that space better, to fill it with what is good, what is just, what will make it better for generations to come, always keeping our eyes on the prize.

14

Since Jim had been education editor for the Statesboro Herald, even when he was not in teaching himself, he was in a position to see many of the changes in education trends, particularly from the administrative point of view. It seemed to him that movement was being made in the "wrong" direction. His philosophy, that education was intended to teach a child how to live, was diametrically opposed to the view rapidly taking over—that education was intended to teach a child how to make a living.

He himself had had a classical education at school, but not in trade skills. He had, for example, taught himself to type. His knowledge of Latin, Greek, German, history, and music gave him a cultural background which enriched his life outside his work.

Job skills had been learned on the job, and he had had several kinds. His summer of Toledo City and recreation work had taught him skills, discipline, and loyalty to his employers. And some of that was learned watching others do it the "wrong" way. I've seen some of that wrong way myself as there are many workers who, being paid by the hour rather than by the job, use company time for themselves or (my very favorite) don't use it at all, just fritter it away. Jim spoke of some of his fellow workers reporting for work, picking up the company truck, then going for breakfast while on the job.

He also learned how not to take up the unhealthy habits of his fellow caddies, smoking heavily and not eating well.

He learned that very few jobs had any training in a formal way—classroom, for example. He felt like an apprentice in many jobs, and I'm sure he was paid that way. Also, he got the most unwanted tasks and time slots. When he was a disc jockey, he was the voice who signed on in the morning, though he did not live in the town where the radio station was located. He spoke often of having to tunnel under houses where all sorts of filth had accumulated for the purpose of repairing or rewiring telephone lines. And this was a job he did for his grandfather-in-law. When he began to coach, he was the one who did all the paper work to get players eligible. He drove the bus to and from events, and he carted home the players whose parents didn't show to pick them up. And I won't even mention his duties as a priest… Oh, wait! I can't. That was confidential, so I didn't hear about any of that. Let me say, though, I am mentioning all of these learning situations, not because Jim complained about them. He literally took them as learning experiences.

No, I mention all this to make a point he made to me and in several of his columns. Once a person has received his basic education—readin', writin,' and 'rithmetic—his job education is mostly received on the job. If his formal high school education is also geared to his job, Jim felt that the student had no preparation for what to do when he was not on the job. He felt that the liberal arts education of literature, history, language, biology, etc., was not just for college prep, but also for life prep. If everybody had the liberal arts education, then everybody's foundation would be similar enough to have common lines of communication between people from all walks of life, then the caste system of "vocational learning" would not prevail.

Quality of life was all-important to Jim, and for that reason, he hated to see "new" proponents throw out everything old just because it was old. He personally said he couldn't get past the on/off switch on the computer, but that didn't keep him from setting up websites and sending out e-mails, though it took him longer because he had to teach himself to do it. I can still see him in his chair at the computer, rotary fan on in addition to the central air, his robe down around his waist because he was hot anyway, working diligently at posting all the volunteer hours for those who had worked at Magnolia Springs State Park during the previous quarter.

He established websites for three different organizations, set up ways to send multiple e-mails to groups he was president of, kept up e-mail communication with friends all over the country and around the world, made birthday cards, downloaded music, etc. And he was old. His inquiring mind was still inquiring at the age of seventy-nine. He was always busy, never lonely, and ever active. I always thought of him as a "Renaissance Man" because he had a well-rounded outlook on his world and his culture.

And he wanted all our school children to have the opportunity for such a diverse education themselves. It wasn't age that presented a barrier between him and young people. He feared it would be the difference in the type of education he and they had had. He advocated for the student's whole life, not just a portion of it.

15

On Education/Pembroke
Jim Hite
Pembroke News, April, 1988

"You Can Lead a Horse to Water…"

Since this is the fifth anniversary of a scathing report on public education in the U.S., entitled "A Nation at Risk," I felt it might be a good time for commentary from the Report.

In "A Nation at Risk," a conclusion was reached that if a foreign nation had done to American education what has been done during the past 30 years or so, this country would consider it an act of war. Most commentators have stated that there are some improvements taking place, and that is true. But there is so much to do and much of it cannot take place overnight, nor is it easily measured.

For example, test scores. They have been rising slowly but surely. However, does that mean our kids are getting smarter, or is it that they are better at taking these particular tests, or…? A couple of weeks back, a news report showed that our best, repeat best, science students ranked from 14th to 17th among 17 nations of the world, including nations in what is termed the "Third World." A news report last Sunday stated that U. S. schools are teaching social skills but may not be doing the job as far as plain, old-fashioned knowledge. It is a real wonder that teachers must have social skills as something they must cover. These should come from the home and only secondarily from the school. But then, what about the home that doesn't do the job.

And that brings another point to the fore. How many parents demand, yes demand, their children work, yes work, for their classes? I wonder. There are some, of course. But so few. Most are concerned if the grades get low, but even these are a small, small minority. And then the accent is on the grades, not the learning. Of course, they go together to a great degree. But education is the goal, not grades.

And we, as a nation, are having trouble defining what education is. Is it training for a job? Is it to be the same for all? Should everyone have the chance for college? Is everyone to be taught courses for college? Should students be chosen for college or other training in other fields early on, or after high school when they think of choosing a career?

Hey, these just scratch the surface. And then I really wonder about how we judge our schools, what standards we hold them to. Is real education brought about by halls of a certain width, rooms of a particular size, new buildings and landscaping, and the like? Maybe these are important! It is obvious that good surroundings make learning easier. But is too much put here? And is all this measuring of education a case of "You scratch my back and I'll scratch yours"? And then I really wonder about teaching and learning having to be "fun." If it is, horrible word, boring... if it demands work... then it is horrible. And if homework is demanded, I'll just forget about it. They'll have to pass me sooner or later, anyway.

Oh, I don't mean to say a class has to be boring. But teachers are often so intimidated that doing something different is a fearful thing. And it must be realized that learning is, for most, just plain work. And this may be the fundamental problem that "A Nation at Risk" and other educators are not facing. To learn takes effort, and that effort includes the student, the teacher, the school, and the home. If one of those is missing, in most instances education will not take place. And if the student just plain does not want to learn, all the gadgets and gimmicks in the world won't do the trick. The old adage holds true: "You can lead a horse to water, but you can't make him (her) drink." And this applies to real learning, called education.

16

On Education
Jim Hite
Millen News, February 20, 2013

"Self-Esteem vs. Learning"
　　While the topic has come up several times over the years, last Sunday as we returned from a weekend in Americus, Joyce and I realized once again how many miles we have traveled together over the past 21 plus years. It is well beyond a million, maybe two, seated next to each other in vehicle or aircraft. Two of our vehicles were traded with over 225,000 miles on the odometer, and we've been shoe-horned into coach seats for cross country and Trans-Atlantic flights as well as one to Mumbai. If you've ever been in coach, you understand such proximity!
　　We realized early on that it's good we like each other!
　　However, there is another part to this equation. We get to talk. So far, we've not run out of topics for discussion, some of them rather heavy, others rather light. Some are topics of agreement, some of disagreement.
　　But they are almost always stimulating.
　　The Americus weekend ended with a 200-mile drive home. Change was our topic. We noticed how many churches had two ser-

vice times on their marquee, one contemporary, one traditional. A change from "what we've always done." We know many churches in Augusta and Statesboro and elsewhere have such a schedule. What a great idea!

We also got into a discussion on education, a frequent topic. We again discussed how the past decades have changed what is termed education. We well remember being told to have the students write, just write. Whatever the course of study, do not correct spelling; do not correct grammar. Just have them express themselves.

The results of this one idea alone are obvious. What used to be typographical errors are just plain errors in spelling and grammar. Spell check is the cure-all. Thus, writing "for witch" when one means "for which" is put in print. Tenses of verbs are all over the place and nominatives are objects of prepositions (read: "for he and I").

Self-esteem is seemingly more important than learning. Students were/are not allowed to fail. Praise and good grades for mediocre (or worse) work have become the norm. Difficulty of study was/is a bad thing.

Then there's the concept that each course needs to be "practical." Learning for its own sake was/is anathema. I have no problem with practical learning. Job skills are basic. And, believe me, I'm sure every youngster in Jenkins County can run rings around me when holding a computer, iPad, notebook, whatever.

But life is more than a job. Life is more than a gadget.

Only learning, lifelong learning provides intellectual stimulation and satisfaction. And the tools for this lifelong endeavor must be provided by our schools.

So much of the blind antagonism and unwillingness to understand those different from us is based on an unwillingness to learn, to educate oneself, to see beyond one's own very little world.

EDUCATE (from Latin *educare*, to bring up a child): To develop and cultivate mentally or morally. (Webster's New Collegiate Dictionary).

A great place from which to start!

17

Religion was another subject Jim wrote columns about. Obviously, he had led a religious life himself, so he was definitely not against it per se. The problem arose, he thought, when people began to worship the church of which they had become members, rather than the God for whom the church had been established.

He had even had that problem in his own church—the Catholic. He had been reared by his parents, primarily his mom, in a pious way. He attended a Catholic school, he sang in a Catholic boys' choir; he served as altar boy in his early life; he attended mass not just on Sunday, but on a daily basis; he observed holy days and fast days with the best of them.

Contrary to what Catholic opponents believe, in his school, he was taught to think. But when thinking led him to veer from the Church's idea of the straight and narrow, thinking led to action, and action led to discipline by the papal hierarchy. He was fine, according to them, as long as he was in seminary, but when he was sent into the world—it was in the '60s after all—he stepped on the toes of Catholic beliefs and mores. Hence, his exile to the farthest reaches of South Georgia. He had loved the hills of North Carolina, the city of Detroit, the beauty of southern Canada, even Baltimore, but he could not be allowed to have influence in any "uptown" areas of Catholic stronghold. So he was assigned the chaplaincy of the state prison in Reidsville, Georgia. Also, he was given churches in three towns – no, I mean one church which served three towns because there were so few Catholics in the area.

This remoteness did prevent his participating in marches and demonstrations about integration and its accompanying fallout, but it did nothing to dull his greatly liberal and forward-thinking beliefs. He had to confine his comments to paper because South Georgia seemed again to be contemplating secession from such a liberal country with its out-of-control Supreme Court.

Even after he left the priesthood, his ideas didn't fit in -- this time with the rank and file of the citizenry of the small town of Pembroke. With his aforementioned desire to get along with everyone, his only option was to curtail his spoken ideas. Not that he gave them up, but they had to be sublimated to other concerns.

Learning to coach and teach school kept him occupied for a while, but sometimes the reins he placed on his tongue slipped and it was made clear to anyone listening where he stood on the value he placed on any life—not just that of members of his own race. That mindset made him ideal for his position of coach in a newly integrated school situation. He even spoke to me later of attending many services in the black churches in the area, making it appear perfectly normal—something a Yankee, a Catholic Yankee, would do.

During that time he became ordained in the Christian Church and was thus able to preach and perform other religious services. He was popular at that because, as a Catholic speaker, he knew the value of the short talk.

After he was ousted from his coaching job (because all the coaches from his school got the boot), he wrote columns for the Pembroke newspaper, then left that position to write for the *Statesboro Herald* for a pittance more. In these columns he was able to write with veiled references to his inner thoughts. He had also by this time returned to services at the Catholic Church.

Even though just by living in the South he had been exposed to the Protestant churches and their way of life, he didn't become embroiled deeply in that outlook until we became a couple. Then we tried to bridge an uncrossable gap. I attended Catholic mass in

Statesboro with him at 8:30 a.m. Sunday mornings, and then we rushed back to Millen to attend my church (the Southern Baptist) and sing in the choir there on a regular basis. These experiences really gave him the chance to see what it was like to live life as narrowly as possible. Thus, he found the personal necessity to come to terms with what his own beliefs really were.

When I had casually mentioned to the then Baptist minister that I was seeing Jim and was serious about him, that person's comment was "Joyce, you don't want any of that!" Oh, but I did! Jim and I became integral parts of both churches—the Baptist and the Catholic. The Sunday School class he attended actually asked him to be their regular teacher, and he accepted until they were shown the error of their ways by someone with Decorum in hand and withdrew their invitation. He became organist for Christmas masses at two of the local Catholic Churches and, as I mentioned, regularly sang in the Baptist Choir, even serving as president for one term.

He was the example we all needed—the person who never had an unkind word for anyone – either to him or about him. One of our friends has mentioned more than once his absolute refusal to say anything uncomplimentary about his ex-wife. He got along with everybody, became fast friends with many, and was the confidant of friends close by and far away.

He read carefully his religious newspapers and articles on line, wrote letters to the editor, and even wrote letters to the authors of some of those articles. He read books on the subject of religion and was especially interested in a book written by the president of Mercer University, a Baptist school at the time. *When We Talk About God, Let's Be Honest* raised a furor in the Baptist church, but received *amens* from Jim.

One of his classmates was an author, and Jim kept up with all of his work, though some was very technical and involved with church theology and opinion. He was also interested in a movement before the beginning of our relationship which had attempted to bring Baptist and Catholic groups into more alignment.

Obviously his columns in the local paper had to be couched in terms that a "sixth grader" could follow (old journalism thought), but his view of the world—not as a "dead and dying" entity, but as a creation of God which would eventually overcome man's tendency to inhumanity—could not be covered up in innocuous language.

His understanding of his own heavenly Father having been called by many names by other God-fearing people transcended the bounds of denominational division. God was God to him, and He was in charge, though we may have tried to box Him into our own ideas of what He should be like.

Our trip to Utah gave him insight into the Mormon culture, and he had difficulty understanding the contrary way Mormons were viewed in South Georgia churches. He stood long and quiet at the foot of the statue of Jesus in the welcome center in Salt Lake City and wondered why other Christians believed Mormons weren't Christian themselves. Aside from the beauty of the temple (from the outside, of course) and the amazing acoustics of the Tabernacle, Jim was also fascinated by the friendliness, helpfulness, and generosity of the citizens. Even our taxi driver became a personal friend.

While there, we visited a cousin of mine whose family was torn within by the polygamy believers and the law-abiding members of that religion. But no matter their beliefs, they were hospitable, and we spent a wonderful afternoon in their home.

And then, with Jim's usual thirst for information, he came home with the Book of Mormon and other reading material Mormons had provided him with and spent much time studying their religion. Not to be outdone, I bought *An Idiot's Guide to Mormonism* and read it cover to cover myself.

In his columns he never allowed his personal bias toward God to cause him to condemn any individual whose beliefs tended toward another form of religion.

Yet he personally felt called to be the best Christian he could be—not just in thought and word, but also in action. And he was deadly serious when he told me that I was being selfish when I refused to accept the position as Sunday School teacher. Obviously I reacted to his comment by becoming the teacher he must have wanted me to become.

He set up automatic payments to many religious charities and left word in his will for his daughter to continue the donations, especially to his mother's old school. But all his charitable thoughts were not reserved for established charitable organizations. If he saw a need and thought he could fill it, he would do so.

My favorite was his presenting some young children between our house and town a new basketball goal because theirs had been broken. Of course, it didn't last long because the neighborhood adults broke it as they had done the previous one, but Jim had done his best.

And that's one thing anybody could say about him. No matter what he believed in, he did it with his whole heart—"all in" as TV announcers are likely to say these days. A genuine example of the once popular WWJD (What Would Jesus Do).

18

On Bigotry
Jim Hite
Millen News, August 18, 2010

"Witch Hunts Are Never Over"

Joyce and I are unabashedly fans of British mysteries. Our DVD collection proves it!

One of our favorites, *Midsomer Murders*, had an episode about individuals murdered following accusations of being witches.

After solving the case, the detective asks if the witch hunts are now over. His daughter responds: "Witch hunts are never over. Ban one, you have to find another! Everyone has to have someone they can feel good about hating."

I taped that statement on my Bible's cover.

For decades, in political, ethnic, and religious spheres, I've found this attitude omnipresent.

Applied to those three spheres, this attitude says my government/country is better than yours, my racial makeup is better than yours, my religion/faith is better than yours.

Therefore, I need to make your government like mine; I am superior to you because of my birth; I have the inside track to heaven and you are lost unless you agree with, worship, and act like me.

This outlook demands my superiority be based on your inferiority. I build myself up by tearing you down.

Possibly, hate may be too strong a word. Maybe it's fear of the unknown, of what is different, a lack of understanding of and appreciation for the differences that exist upon God's good earth.

Apply it across the above three spheres. We're seeing it played out in the growth of confrontational politics, especially during the past two decades, where tearing down the other is part and parcel of the political process rather than working for the common good. We're seeing it in "ethnic cleansing" that has gone on for centuries and continues to this very day, becoming so much a part of world events we have become oblivious to its presence. We've seen it in religion for centuries as well, where some Christians were so positive they had the only way to salvation that they killed "heretics" to save their souls! Many have not learned from history. We still have Christian denominations convinced their way is the only way and all other Christians, let alone non-Christians, are "lost." We still have conflicts centuries and millennia old in the Middle East where war continues, each party self-assured that God is on its side.

All these are things we do so we can feel good about hating another.

I read the Midsomer quote almost daily. It's a constant reminder to keep close watch on my attitude as well as my tongue, hopefully to catch myself if I ever even begin to "feel good" about any attitude that denigrates another person's birthplace, ethnic background, or approach to God.

19

Jim and I watched a great deal of TV. But we were not slaves to the TV schedule, thanks to today's taping advances. Many times the night shows were our lunchtime fare for the next day. We especially liked murder mysteries and cop shows. I must have been an aggravating co-watcher because nearly always I figured out who the villain was too soon. Every time I was right (that I had announced), Jim would ask, "When are you going to start writing for TV? That way we could make some money, and I wouldn't have to worry any more about my stock portfolio."

Jim wrote column after column for the Millen News, before that for the Statesboro Herald and the Pembroke newspaper. So my question was, "When are you going to compile all of this material and publish it?" Obviously neither of us acted on the urging of the other to write.

However, we did discuss the writing of the "book." Jim was going to write about his childhood, and I would write about mine. Then we'd put it together the best way it made sense. Well, Jim blew it. He wrote letters and grants and projects, but he never got around to writing about himself. That's why, in this book, I'm taking on things about his childhood, his high school time, his seminary days, and his first marriage. It is not according to our collaborative plan.

When we first dated and drove to races as far away as Mississippi, when we went in his little Subaru "LUV" truck, I'd sit on the passenger side but facing him, and he would talk on and on. But it was mostly about happy times. If something unpleasant came up, he would become reticent, almost close-mouthed.

His discussions were philosophical sometimes, but he loved telling anecdotes about specific events in his life. And those I remember well. I may not have the chronology right, but where we were when he remembered something and the circumstances surrounding his telling, I do remember. And of course, since the anecdotes were not told in any specific order, I don't remember them in any orderly logical framework.

He spoke more than once of how the river—the Maumee, I presumed—became so polluted that it caught on fire.

He talked about his mother's constant diligence where others were concerned. She'd say, repeatedly, "What will people think?"

The one time he answered her with "People don't think of you as often as you think they do" did not win him any parental approval.

He spoke of walking with his daddy down to the railroad tracks; the big yard was only a few blocks from their home. His dad had also hawked sandwiches and drinks on the train as a child.

He talked of his dad's being discriminated against on the job because he was Irish Catholic. And during World War II his mom's family felt the same type of discrimination because they were German.

He spoke of being drafted as a child to "chaperon" his cousin Rose on her dates with Tom. Later Rose and Tom married and raised six children—all adopted and none from like families. Rose was the one to find his mother and call Jim about her death.

His experience as a safety monitor and crossing guard drew chuckles from his mom later in their lives. That he would be considered "safe" was foreign to her.

He spoke of his childhood friends with whom he tried to reconnect after his mother's death. While she was alive, she wanted him to herself when he visited Toledo, and that left no time to socialize unless those he was socializing with came to her house.

He spoke about having lived in Cleveland in his very young childhood, so young he had only vague memories of it.

But the family had had two homes in Toledo, not many blocks apart. When we ran there, we ran between the two and around by Jean and Tom's and by his grandmother's home.

I was fascinated when he talked of his Sundays at home in Toledo. Mass was always first on the agenda, and then there was the ride around with grandmother and Uncle Bernie, wearing the hot wool clothes and eating out at the automat-style cafeteria.

They did travel some because he spoke of a car trip through Georgia at least once. He didn't remember much about it except the pathetic dwellings by the main highways—US 25 for him—straight from Toledo through Millen.

He wore uniforms to his Catholic school and for much of his early childhood heavy corrective shoes as he had been born with club feet, and the shoes were to teach his feet proper walking methods.

Uncle Bernie must have exerted some influence on Jim in his early thinking years. Again I'm vague about the facts about Uncle Bernie, but I know he offered to pay for Jim's schooling as long as Jim worked hard to earn as much as possible—and he did. He worked at B. R. Baker's men's clothing store, he jumped deliveries on a florist's truck, he was a caddy at Heatherdowns Country Club, and he worked maintenance for the city of Toledo. And Uncle Bernie held up his end of the bargain. I have the impression that he had himself studied to be a priest, but it didn't happen, perhaps because of his obsessive-compulsive disorder. He dealt in stocks instead, and he didn't end well—suicide, I'm thinking. But his stocks did.

I did not know of Jim's being a cheerleader in high school until I attended a class reunion with him—awkward because he had also taken his first wife to one of the reunions. He was great friends with the ball-players (basketball)—one in particular—Dennis O'Shea whom we visited more than once in Denver, Colorado.

Jim didn't start running races until 1978, but he ran every time he went home to visit. He spoke of a race so cold his beard (yes, he had one when he worked for the phone company) froze. He talked about running across the "high-level" bridge, so our second trip to

Toledo we did just that, but it was a scary adventure. The snow plows had taken care of the roads, but the sidewalks on the bridge were piled high, so it was mainly just picking our way across. It was more adventurous and less tiring than our first run there had been the summer before. On that occasion we had set out late in the afternoon for a five-mile loop he was very familiar with. And though I was really not as fast as he was at that short a distance, I couldn't let him show me up. When we had been running—dodging traffic when we had to leave sidewalks and going single file at his insistence (which meant we were not really running together)—for what seemed to me at least four and a half miles, we were stunned by the sign in the middle of the road—*Detour* Bridge Out. There was no shortcut that even he knew back to his mother's house, so we had to retrace our steps, in oncoming darkness, for another four and a half miles. His mother's house had a room on the second floor and a basement. He showed me the "upper room" proudly, for it had been his inner sanctum when he had lived there and it was where he had his ham radio setup. He spoke of people he had communicated with from all over the country. Showing me the basement was a necessity as that was where the shower was located—a gloomy, dark green painted stall which both of us had to use as the ground floor bathroom was set up for a handicapped person. Not that his mother was handicapped, but the paraphernalia was precautionary.

That was the house on Durango; most of his memories were from Woodsdale where he had a basketball goal in his backyard and a school yard across the street where he and the neighborhood children met to play. I don't remember discussions of girls joining that play. I remember two girls he talked about, however, during his (and their) high school years. One was a great golfer and was later on the LPGA circuit and one other he had dated a few times, though with no future in mind. His mother already had his future planned.

One of his biggest memories from high school has to be the production of *HMS Pinafore*. Central Catholic staged it with one of his fellow students directing. Not just all the rehearsals or just the performances, but the "after" party really captured his memory. I guess it was the skinny dipping in Lake Erie that piqued his imagination.

He was also very proud of Toledo's city parks, so Swan Creek became one of our regular haunts when we didn't choose just to run from Durango. Just as he'd had to put up with my whining the day we went too far, now he had to listen to my squeals because the snow plows didn't clear the paved trail; after all, it was a preserved natural park.

The trips he took on the train to basketball games were memorable to him, too. Those, coupled with his daddy's attraction to trains and his own train trips to and from Seminary (though these were few), are probably the root of his deep-seated love for trains and enjoyment of watching them shuttle back and forth at the railroad yard. He's the only person I ever heard say when approaching a railroad track, "Oh, goody. We get to wait for the train."

So when his daughter Jody had a resident at the retirement community (where she was activities director) who, because of his dementia, was destroying his N gauge train layout, Jim borrowed a van and drove it all the way to Raleigh to retrieve a very unwieldy construction monstrosity. He spent many entertaining hours getting it put up and operating, so he could display it to his grandson Patrick and his friends.

His memories of his cousin Fritz were heart-tugging. Apparently Fritz had been one of his childhood idols. He had been a pilot in World War II, had seen consistent fighting over Germany, and had managed to get completely through the war unscathed. But when he was taking a little vacation before coming back to America, he went down. Jim was heart-broken at the time, and talking about it always brought tears to his eyes. I'm sure that's why on all our travels for races, he always looked for military landmarks. When we went for his World Duathlon in Belgium, he looked up online and found the burial place of a close school friend's brother. We were there on Memorial Day, and our trip across the border to Maastricht in Germany put us at a cemetery where a Memorial ceremony was being held. It was attended by living veterans of the campaign and sponsored by the citizens of Germany and Belgium who had adopted graves of Americans who had given their lives in World War II. Jim took pictures of the gravesite of his friend. When he told the brother of the buried soldier what he had found, the response was "Oh, that's nice." Jim, on the other hand, had cried throughout the ceremony. I lasted until the missing plane formation flew over before I broke down as well.

When we were in Hawaii, he wanted to visit Pearl Harbor—twice; when I told him my dad had served on Guam, he bought me a video about the campaign there.

And he was really a student of the Civil War. When we were in Manassas, Virginia, he wasn't happy until we drove all around the battlefields. We had to visit Appomattox Courthouse where Lee surrendered. In Chickamauga, Georgia, he drove all around the battle areas, coming dangerously close to the marathon runners on the course through the same area. When we were on the shore of Lake Erie, he took me to the burial place of Confederate soldiers who had died while in prison on Johnson Island there. He was steeped in all the history surrounding Camp Lawton in Millen and was so very proud to be named the first president of Friends of Magnolia Springs State Park and to be honored by the Jenkins and Screven County group of Sons of Confederate Veterans. He was their favorite "Damn Yankee."

As anyone knows who has tried to change careers and teach in the state of Georgia, no amount of education makes any difference unless you've had the prescribed courses—prescribed by the Georgia Department of Education. So though Jim had the equivalent of more than a doctor of philosophy degree, he had to almost start over in college to be able to be certified to teach in Georgia. Being new to the state, he felt he should know Georgia history, and that's when he became acquainted with Dr. Todd, who recognized Jim's "Renaissance Man" education and said so. She was a student of the South, and she won Jim over with her Southern genteel ways. He taught Georgia history then and visited every monument he could, talking about each of them nonstop. We visited Civil War sites I was not sure I'd ever heard of.

Suffice it to say, that whatever Jim tried, he tried it to the very best of his ability. Whatever he signed on for, he went above and beyond in attempting to carry it out. And he enjoyed the trying. It was as if he owed God for his life and he wanted to make God glad He had created him. He wanted to be the best father. He wanted to be the best coach. He wanted to be the best humanitarian, the kind nobody knew about. He wanted to be the best teacher. He even wanted to be the best horseback rider—horse frolic with its clover-leaf timed races and other wild adventures. He wanted to be the best softball player.

When he began running, he won his first race—I heard in a pair of women's shorts—so after that, not running his fastest from the gun was not an option, a trait he shared with Steve Prefontaine whose pictures still bedeck the walls of our home. That's why marathoning was not for him; pacing is hard for somebody with a sprint mindset.

He wanted to love and be loved, so though he had strong principles and stood by them, he tried to be pleasant and to get along with people whose ideas were not compatible with his. That winsome smile of his could win anybody over, and since he used it often and sincerely, he did win everybody over. It would be hard to count just the service people that he dealt with who appreciated him enough to say so and to put it in writing.

One example is Hazel Gibbs, the usher on the fourth tier up in Atlanta Braves Stadium where Georgia Games gave us seats for helping with the track meet. She called her section "Hazel's Haven," and though I'm sure Jim was not her only project, his grateful attitude made him one of her favorites. He had met her only twice, but when I went back to a game in 2014, she cried at his loss and has written me several times since.

There are many others, some of whom I don't know by name—waitresses, janitors, gas station attendants—they were all people to him, and they deserved his thanks and his praise.

He befriended athletes, coaches, and officials from all over the world. One of the pictures on my digital frame was taken in Ottawa with two of his fellow competitors from Great Britain.

Our handlers in India speak of him fondly. And the wait staff at that five-star Trident Hotel in Mumbai gathered for him to take their picture. Our *maître d'* at the Hyde Park hotel in London offered to carry out all sorts of errands for him and did so without accepting a tip. And there's the bus driver in one of the outskirts of London who helped us find an overgrown field to cut through to get to a race on time.

He had three travel agents over the years who loved him dearly. One in particular we'd only actually seen once, but over the years their phone conversations about the places we were going, what we would do there, and the arrangements for accommodations sounded like two bosom friends catching up on old times. Then though she was not on the immediate call list, when she read Jim's obituary in the paper, she drove eighty miles alone to come to his funeral ceremony.

Every year, Jim sent Christmas cards to numerous people from his early years whose connections with him I was not clear about. Many were neighbors, some were distant relatives, some were high school classmates, and some were fellow seminarians. But once he had established a connection, he hated to lose it.

There are many facts I could possibly chase down about Jim's past, but this writing is not an exposé. It is merely my cobbled-together impressions of a man whose life touched that of many, and to this day, I have heard of no one whose life was harmed in any way by that touch. As a matter of fact, I'm still marveling that I was fortunate enough to spend twenty-three years with him.

As I said, he threatened to write his life story, but he only got so far as to make outlines of the things he thought were important to whatever theme he was working on. And each time he started, he would lay the project aside because to him it sounded like boasting. Listing of his accomplishments always put somebody else first—the teams he coached, the groups he led, the organizations he chaired, his own children and grandchildren, his students, my grandchildren, and me.

In a world where "I" is the most important pronoun, Jim's motto was "you" first. He was proud of what he'd been able to accomplish, but he was more proud of the letters he received from folks who recognized those things he'd been successful in.

Separately both of us had made marks in the worlds of education, running, administration of running and other events, music, and church work. But together our influence had more than a single facet each. Together we made the whole stone—a diamond, I hope.

And when I look back on our time together, that "wrong way" does not speak merely of direction, of different lifestyle, of different viewpoints, but of different attitudes about the same experiences others have. His *you* philosophy changed me and many others he touched.

Jim with two of his British competitors in
Ottawa one month before his death

20

On Aging
Jim Hite
Millen News, July 10, 2013

"Tenacity as We Grow Older"

As my "running" career continues, it seems I hear the phrase "Hang in there!" more frequently. Of course, it may be my imagination. But then again, it may be that some astute observers notice my struggle to put one foot in front of the other at a pace I need in order to train and thus take part credibly in various competitions.

Months short of completing my eighth decade on earth, I have seen the time it takes me to cover specific distances lengthen noticeably. Finish times in races are now more than double what they were when I was running my fastest over 30 years ago. And to be honest, going slower today is much more of a struggle than the faster training and racing of times long past.

But as Ray Miller says when we get together for our twice-weekly morning runs: "We're out here!" And he is kind enough to slow down so we can run together.

A couple of weeks ago, on the Mormon Tabernacle Choir's program "Music and the Spoken Word," the words were about *tenacity*. The speaker noted the word derives from the Latin for "hold fast."

I thought: "There's a column here!"

That word is a good description of "Hang in there."

You may or may not agree, but I think we can base daily living, especially as we grow older, on that one word. Just as an athlete must hold on all the way to the finish line, so we must continue to live, to hold on and realize that the agony of defeat comes only from quitting.

Far too many quit living even as they continue breathing. Vibrancy is gone, replaced by negativity, a critical and narrow attitude, a personality that repels rather than attracts.

Such as these have taken the easy way. Just as it is much easier to stay in an easy chair than get out the door and move, so it is much easier to quit and close one's self to mental and spiritual growth.

I appreciate those of you who are so encouraging as I shuffle, jog, run (choose your description) the roads of Jenkins County. I hope I can continue to my last day. As we have been running for several decades, Joyce and I have several friends (who were friends through running) who are now dead. They did not stop until the body could go no more. Many were "out there" until their last days whether in their seventh, eighth, or ninth decade.

They were vibrant, positive, attractive, open, and a pleasure to be with. Not one of them quit!

They were great models of real living.

They had tenacity!

21

Everything has a beginning, a middle, and an end, I guess, but in our case we didn't know the middle was the middle, so the end couldn't really be that. It is true that Jim had retired from two or three of his volunteer projects, but several of them were ongoing. I have tried to keep those alive, but of course, some I could not. The first thing I had to do was to cancel a speaking engagement he had set up for Tuesday following his death on Friday. I wouldn't have minded a speaking engagement, but the topic was Revolutionary War history of this area, for which he had carried out exhaustive research.

Another project of his (and of Millen Milers and More) was a new race to replace our cross country race at Magnolia Springs State Park. The very day he died he had placed an ad in Running Journal magazine announcing the fastest 5K—certified—in the area. It was supposed to be on the runway at the Jenkins County Airport. A few days after his death MMM was informed that the FAA would not allow the runway to be closed for an hour for the race. Jim would have been devastated, but luckily, he never had to find out about that cancellation. Fortunately, also, we had already announced at the 2012 Magnolia race that it was the last one of that series.

But he was still president of two organizations and a member of several others. One was Friends of Magnolia Springs State Park. He had been its first president and had never been succeeded. That organization is still operative, and Jim was so proud to have been associated with it at the time of the discoveries about Camp Lawton, the Confederate prison at the end of the Civil War. He was working diligently on a joint project with Johnson Island, a Union prison camp in Lake Erie which we had toured on one of our trips to Ohio to visit Jim's mother. Not wanting to accept the leadership role and fail him in any way, I became secretary of the group.

Another was presidency of the Augusta Choral Society Council where he was liaison between singers, leadership, and sponsors of that organization. He was meticulously organized so that handing his notes over to the new chairman was a simple job. Here again, I retained my position as secretary for the council.

Trying to maintain his position in other groups was not always possible, but I have made an attempt. In his church (St. Bernadette in Millen) I have attended at least once a quarter, and I have made his birthday contributions. I can't, however, play the organ at Midnight mass on Christmas Eve, and I don't believe I'm allowed to do the readings as I am not Catholic. His classmates at Central Catholic High School (those who are still living) keep me in contact, and we exchange Christmas cards as he did year after year. Some of his priest colleagues still check with me, and one (Bob Hater) took me to lunch when I ran the Flying Pig Marathon in Cincinnati.

He had no close relatives—the Ohio ones—left, but Bill, the cousin we visited in France, e-mails me occasionally. And he and his children send Christmas cards as well. Bill's sister Mary Kate lives in Toledo, and in the spring of 2015, when I fulfilled a promise to Jim that I would visit the graves of his parents, I called her for information as I had forgotten the name of the cemetery.

Jim had rotated out of his position on the State Board of the Georgia Retired Educators Association, but other members and retired teachers from his area—Augusta, Vidalia, Savannah, and Brunswick—remember him to me often. Just last week one lady who didn't know me was asking about Jim's death and remarking on his contribution to that organization.

The Atlanta Track Club, whose board he served on for eight years, has changed policies of the track team, but when I attend track meets, I am recognized as Jim's wife and heralded to be out there running and getting points for the team. Opponents in his age group, Ken Ogden and Jerry Levasseur from California for two, spoke of him just this summer as being fast. I tell him he has become faster in his absence. A steeplechaser, Doug Smith from Toronto, who had not heard of his death, burst into tears upon hearing of it the following summer. Dr. Brian Hickey, another steeplechaser and duathlete, professor at FAMU, was also distraught.

Jim also certified courses for USA Track and Field, and race directors still call asking for help in that very challenging operation. But that was a three-man job, and though I may give some answers, I can't carry out the whole process.

Jim's daughter Jody has been a brick. He and she had an established pattern of phone calls every Sunday night and every Wednesday night. I can't call her on those nights—they're sacrosanct. But any other time, whether she's at work or at play, she welcomes hearing from me.

My granddaughter Chelsea has helped me more than she knows. She was not old enough to go on as many trips with Jim and me as her older sisters, but she has made up for it by going with me, sometimes as a volunteer helper at races, sometimes just to be company. The year following Jim's death, she came to my sister's funeral to support me in case my emotions took over and I couldn't finish my remarks. Jim never forgot and often quoted a line she used once when we were discussing something she considered trivial: "It matters *not!*" It seemed to sum up his own thoughts on idle talk.

Though Jim Hite liked to keep up with what was going on around him, locally and far-reaching, his methods of unearthing information did not resemble his neighbors'. For instance, his radio listening was confined to NPR stations with their in-depth news. (Unless the Braves were playing, of course.) His television watching was primarily the History channel. His newspaper reading was the USA Today. His days of gathering info at the morning coffee klatsch, of chewing the fat with the good ole' boys, and watching local TV stations were left behind upon his retirement. Once he discovered the internet, he did read a couple of magazines and his hometown paper—the Toledo Blade—on line, so he probably knew more about what was happening in Ohio than in Georgia. And he didn't use Facebook to find out about friends and family.

But he continued to write letters—to relatives, to close friends, to people he had met and wanted to keep in contact with. And apparently, they wanted the same thing. Luckily he didn't have to depend on letters from them, but phone calls and e-mails kept them connected.

Though we lived in the country outside a small town, he was, as he put it, a citizen of the world—not just of our town, our state, or even our country. Like E. M. Forster's "cloud," the people he knew were a palpable presence in his life, in his thoughts, in his words, and in his actions.

And those were transparent. He told me once when we were dating, "What you see is what you get." He meant he didn't lie, and I found that to be true. He didn't even equivocate. Sometimes in his columns when I was proofreading, I would add or subtract a word to make his ideas more palatable to our community, but he never tried to mislead anyone.

And, as for actions, if his "right" way was the "wrong" way, so be it. He lived his life the best way he knew how, and I'm glad to have been a part of it.

In this volume I've included some of his columns and excerpts from others, so you don't have to take my word alone for what he was thinking.

Today I find myself quoting those thoughts of his—to myself, to my sons, to my grandchildren, to his daughter, and to our friends. For they are good thoughts and worthy to be remembered.

Our last Christmas card – Ottawa 8/11/2013

About the Author

Joyce Hodges-Hite is a retired school teacher from Georgia who felt that the story of her relationship with Jim Hite needed to be told. Jim was the one who had continued to write beyond his school years, though Joyce had always considered herself a writer. Both had taught English (with her a preference; with him a necessity), but she turned out to be more of a proofreader.

During her school years, she had been editor of her high school and her college newspaper and advisor to two student papers. Her only writing (other than assignments) included a few short stories and a teaching career memoir.

Since Jim's death, she has continued many of their involvements: singing in a symphonic choir (serving as an officer of the council) in a city fifty miles away; officiating at track meets and road races in two states; being a church member in a Southern Baptist church, albeit with an objective look at some of its practices; and *running*.

Admittedly a middle-of-the-packer even in her winning days, she is experiencing success today by completing the races she enters, hopefully making Jim happy in his heavenly overview of her activities. Her looming eightieth birthday in 2017 was also his goal, but he fell short of it.

She, however, is still busily making plans for it.

CPSIA information can be obtained
at www.ICGtesting.com
Printed in the USA
LVOW03s0608190717

541482LV00001B/42/P